MARGARET BAKER

DISCOVERING CHRISTMAS CUSTOMS AND FOLKLORE

A guide to seasonal rites

SHIRE PUBLICATIONS LTD

British Library Cataloguing in Publication Data: Baker, Margaret. Discovering Christmas Customs and Folklore: Guide to Seasonal Rites — 3 rev. ed. — (Discovering Books; No. 32). I. Title. II. Series. 394.2. ISBN 0-7478-0175-4.

Cover: *The modern image of Santa Claus or Father Christmas is largely founded on this illustration by Thomas Nast, published in Harper's Illustrated Weekly in 1863 (see chapter 7).*

Printed in Great Britain by C. I. Thomas & Sons (Haverfordwest) Ltd, Press Buildings, Merlins Bridge, Haverfordwest, Dyfed SA61 1XF.

2

THE SEASON AND ITS CUSTOMS

The Twelve Days

The Christmas season is variously defined. Ecclesiastically, it runs from Advent to Candlemas (2nd February). The old Twelve Days of Christmas (Christmas Eve to Epiphany, 6th January) are still remembered, if mostly in carols. Under the old agricultural calendar a long holiday at a season of little work was possible but today for practical reasons Christmas has shrunk and usually means the period from midnight on 24th December to New Year's Day.

There are many variations. In Denmark, Norway and Sweden Christmas lasts from St Lucia's Day (13th December) until St Knut's Day (13th January), when the Christmas tree is dismantled to the pleasant wish:

> May God bless your Christmas
> May it last till Easter.

A Czech Christmas starts on *Svatej* (6th December) and ends at *Tri Kralu*, Three Kings' Day (6th January). In Italy, from the beginning of the Novena (the eight days preceding Christmas) until Epiphany, children recite for coins. The Twelve Days in Ireland ended with *Nollaig naMban* or 'Women's Christmas', distinct from *Nollaig na bhFear*, 'Men's Christmas'.

Until the eighteenth century the Twelve Days ruled — 'England's twelve dayes' madness', wrote one poet. On Lake District farms all work, except for animal care, ceased. The spinning wheel was silent; the flail hung idle on the wall; people went from house to house feasting, singing, dancing. Every neighbour in turn was visited; the Christmas pie and the home-brewed ale possets were the proud preoccupation of every housewife.

The 'Twelfths' had strict rules. Spinning, the prime occupation for women, was forbidden and distaffs (on which wool or flax was wound) were ceremonially bound up with flowers to prevent their use. North German housewives knew that supernaturals were about and that flax left out would be spitefully tangled by ill-disposed Woden, Frau Gode or Frau Holde. In Denmark and Oldenburg, Germany, no wheel turned, whether for spinning or for farm work. To bake invited attention from the Wild Hunt and kitchen doors were kept tightly shut lest the huntsmen creep into the house and take up malevolent residence for the whole year.

Certain Christmas customs are still linked with the calendar changes of 1752, when, under the act of Parliament *24 Geo II* the Gregorian (New Style) calendar replaced the Julian (Old Style) in

Britain and America. In September 1752 eleven days were omitted from the calendar, to the consternation of some who felt — falsely — that they had been deprived of rightful life. ('Give us back our eleven days,' howled the mob.) 25th December became Christmas Day (New Style) and 6th January Christmas Day (Old Style) or Old Christmas Day. New and old dates may still conflict and confusion lingers, even after 250 years.

Advent and its wreath

The four weeks of Advent, which precede Christmas, are a period of grace-giving preparation for the greatest of Christian festivals. Holy candles are lighted with joyful expectancy in home and church. Cribs are readied. It is an emotional contemplative period of waiting for the Lord, with a pervasive sense of the supernatural.

During Advent in southern Germany *Klöpfelnächte* (Knocking Nights) accentuate this strangeness. Mummer-like figures run from house to house, singing, knocking on doors with rods and throwing pebbles, crying the Lord's coming and wishing neighbours well. With civil treatment the visitors could be induced to dance on the fields. Was the original intention to drive away evil with the din or to confirm neighbours' luck? Primitive origins must be suspected. In the sixteenth century Naogeorgus explained it thus:

> Three weekes before the day whereon was borne the Lord of Grace,
> And on the Thursdaye Boyes and Girles do runne in every place,
> And bounce and beate at every doore, with blowes and lustie snaps,
> And crie, the Advent of the Lorde not borne as yet perhaps,
> And wishing to the neighbours all, that in the houses dwell,
> A happie yeare, and every thing to spring and prosper well.

As curious are the Berchtesgaden (Bavaria) figures of *Nikolo-Weibl*, a boy dressed as a girl, who attends St Nicholas, and the twelve *Buttenmandln*, young men in animal masks, skins and cowbells. Noisily they tramp with St Nicholas from house to house early in Advent. The saint preaches and gifts are given, but then the cast changes and the *Buttermandln* roister forth and fall on the young people present. Treatment may be boisterous but the blows, pre-Christian in origin and luck-bringing, are accepted in good part.

In the German-speaking countries the Advent wreath (*Advent-kranz*) is common. Wreaths are usually decorated with four red candles, one for each Advent Sunday, or the candles may be set in a wooden candlestand, to be lighted as the weeks pass.

Typically, amid houses brilliantly lighted for the season, a huge Advent wreath hangs on the town fountain in the square at Berchtesgaden (and there is an Advent wreath society promoting it). Thousands of fir wreaths are to be seen all over Germany and Austria. Lufthansa German Airlines hangs evergreens in the cabins of its aircraft during Advent. The liking for the round, sun-symbol, red-ribboned door wreath in the United States, fast spreading to Britain, perhaps was prompted by Advent wreaths; in Czechoslovakia the wreath hangs on the Christmas tree.

Children may be given candles marked with 24 divisions, one to be burned on each day of Advent until Christmas Eve. Advent calendars, too, are popular. A cardboard house in a frosted landscape may have 24 small glowing windows to open, day by day; or an embroidered pendant tapestry may offer 24 tiny parcels for the child to open, revealing sweets or a charm for each day on the spiritual road to Christmas.

The Christchild's Market

The *Christkindlesmarkt* (Christchild's Market) or *Weihnachtsmarkt* (Christmas Market) in the market squares of Germany and Austria from early Advent to Christmas Eve express the historic German Christmas tradition.

The most famous *Christkindlesmarkt* (dating from 1639) is held in Nuremberg. Simple wooden booths, roofed with red and green striped awnings, are garlanded with fir branches, lanterns and streamers and surround the crib with wooden figures in the centre of the Hauptmarkt. The emotional opening ceremony of the Prologue, spoken from the Frauenkirche balcony by the 'Christchild', newly elected every two years, the carols, the children's procession with home-made lanterns to see the living Christmas tableaux at the Castle and events in the churches are part of every Nuremberg Christmas. Most romantically, the scene, beloved of children, will be seen through the first whirling flakes of snow and as dusk falls the stalls light their lanterns and the church and late fourteenth-century *Schöner Brunnen* (Beautiful Fountain) glow in the soft light.

Goods are for Christmas use, as well as those purely intended as presents: fruit and vegetables, local foods, Christmas-tree decorations, small wooden toys (with four hundred toy factories, Nuremberg is the toy capital of the world), tin soldiers, wooden nutcrackers, trinkets, small glass and brass objects, candles, gingerbread figures. Everywhere wafts the delicious smell of the famous Nuremberg pork sausages grilled over beechwood — *Nürnberger Bratwürste*. The equally famous *Rauschgoldengel*, made of finely pleated gold paper foil, perhaps deriving from the Christchild and from the Angel of the Annunciation and almost a symbol of German Christmas itself, greets all visitors. The original winged and armless figure is based on the costumes of the eighteenth century; a modern variation, the Nuremberg *Weihnachtsengel* (Christmas Angel), is of wax with baroque robes, feathered wings and a candlestick in its raised hand. Other specialities are the little figures of *Zwetschgenmännle* or 'Prune Men', made of dried prunes and crêpe paper.

Local foods are always important in Christmas markets: in Brunswick, Germany, fishcakes, in Aachen, Germany, *Printen* biscuits; in Lübeck, Germany, marzipans. In Gouda, Holland, huge cheeses are rolled on carts to a candlelit festival. Berlin prepares to enjoy candy floss and roasted almonds. In Nuremberg *Glühwein*, roast chestnuts, and more of the incomparable pork sausages keep the cold out.

A brilliantly lighted night-time view of the annual Christkindlesmarkt in the Hauptmarkt, Nuremberg, Germany. The Christchild speaks the opening prologue from the balcony of the Frauenkirche in the background. On the left is the fourteenth-century fountain, 'Schöner Brunnen'. (Stadt Nürnberg.)

Lebkuchen, small spice cakes or biscuits with honey, nuts and spices, have been associated with Nuremberg as long as the market. *Lebkuchen* making is said to have prospered in Nuremberg because the city's forests provided excellent honey and its merchants a reliable supply of spices. *Lebkuchen* are particularly associated with Christmas.

The city of Liège, Belgium, has a December *Village de Noël* in the Place de Marché, the heart of the city, facing the town hall and surrounding the Crib. Fir-decked booths sell such goods as *santons* ('little saints'), candles, garlands and characteristic foods: fresh salmon, oysters, pâtés, cheeses, chocolates, *viandes séchées* (dried meats) and *boudins de Noël* (black puddings). To accompany the foods are mulled wine, vodka, the powerful *bières de Noël* and Pèkêt dè Houyeu, a great speciality, used to flame the *bouquette de Noël*. Entertainment is wide-ranging, including music and choral singing of all kinds, marionettes, for which Liège is famous, clowns, miming, folk music, jazz and dancing. Four thousand balloons are given away to children.

'Christmas stores', emporia with large car parks, open all the year to sell Christmas goods, are dotted across the United States. Whole rooms are often devoted to videos and tableaux with themes such as 'The Christmas Carol' and 'The Alpine Room'. Costumes, masks, decorations, crackers, lights, records and tapes are sold, there are even massive displays of paper hats and that American perennial, the striped candy cane, to be found on every Christmas tree.

Christmas shops can be found in Britain also, and include those at Chester, York, Bath, Stratford-upon-Avon, London and Windsor. All stock traditional Christmas toys and goods. Typical is the Christkindlmarkt in Canterbury, with such items as the Bozen singing angel, candle in hand, of clay pressed in an old wooden mould; Advent candlestands; Crib figures; wooden nutcrackers and 'Smoky Man', a German Christmas toy of some lineage, which can look suspiciously like Father Christmas and which puffs out fragrant Christmas smoke.

Boy bishops

The election of the mock 'boy bishop' or 'St Nicholas's bishop', now defunct except in occasional revivals, but once familiar in England, France and Germany, was perhaps another link with Saturnalian role-changing. In cathedrals, choir schools or parish churches, in a ceremony both sacred and burlesque, a choirboy proclaimed 'bishop' wore the full vestments of a genuine prelate from 6th December, St Nicholas's Day, until 28th December, Holy Innocents. The 'bishop' might preach and perform all a bishop's

11

offices except mass. Should such a boy die in office he was buried with full honours; Salisbury Cathedral, Wiltshire, has an effigy of a 'boy bishop' who died in such circumstances. The custom was suppressed by Henry VIII in 1542 and died out after the death of Mary I. The tradition lasted longer in Europe but vanished in the eighteenth century. The ceremony in Zug, Switzerland, was stopped in 1797 to protests from every side.

The effigy in Salisbury Cathedral, Wiltshire, of the boy bishop who died in office. He would have received an episcopal funeral.

The Feast of St Lucia

In Sweden 13th December is celebrated as the Feast of St Lucia. Traditionally at cockcrow, when it is still dark, the youngest daughter of the house, wearing a white robe with a red sash and a wire crown decorated with whortleberry twigs and supporting nine lighted candles, and carrying a tray of coffee and cakes — known as *Lussekake*, greets the household. She wakes the sleepers, sings her song to them and is proclaimed *Lussi* or *Lussibruden* (Lucy Bride).

In a brilliantly lighted room breakfast is then served, with separate rations for the family's animals. Lights are the hallmarks of this festival. At one time shooting and fishing by torchlight were amusements of the day. In west Gotland Lussi visited neighbours' houses, stables, barns and cow byres, her procession accompanied by torchbearers, maids of honour, biblical characters, and trolls and demons defeated by the reviving sun.

Nothing in Lucia's story connects her with light. But, significantly, under the Old Style 13th December was the winter solstice, when sun magic was appropriate. Midwinter pleasure at the turn of the year is still a strong emotion; today the St Lucia custom has become so popular that it has left its purely domestic setting. Parishes, villages, clubs, schools and companies all gather to choose their own Lussis.

Candles and customs

Enhancing the mystery of Christmas Eve in Berchtesgaden, Bavaria, a lighted candle is placed at every grave. Candles make a glowing carpet in the snow round the old church of Oddense, Kristiansand, Norway, and in rural Ireland a large candle burns in every kitchen window on Christmas Eve and smaller ones in other windows to honour the Holy Family who sought shelter and as a beacon for the lonely and homeless.

Until the late nineteenth century old-fashioned grocers in England gave their customers a complimentary pair of gigantic Yule candles as a Christmas present, one red and one blue. They approached the Yule log in ritual importance. They had to be a gift, never a purchase, and were lighted and extinguished only by the head of the household. Such candles stood burning steadily in the middle of the table, never to be moved or snuffed, lest death follow. The Yule candle, wreathed in greenery, must burn through Christmas night until the sun rose or the Christmas service began. In Norway two candles burned every evening until New Year's Day; like the Yule log their light shed blessings and increase on all it touched: clothes, food, animals or family silver.

Even wax leftovers came in useful. A cross marked with Yule wax on animals' backs on Christmas morning ensured their health or an enhanced milk yield. Wax crumbs in the hens' feeding dish meant many eggs. Before spring ploughing Swedish ploughs were smeared with Yule candle grease and in Denmark Yule wax burned protectively in thunderstorms.

Wassailing the apple trees

In the cider districts of the west and south-west of England farmers once wassailed their apple orchards to waken the sleeping tree spirits to their duty and provide a good crop. The ritual survives tenuously as a pub custom in cider areas on Twelfth Night or Old Twelfth Night. The farmer, his family and men visited the orchards at dusk with lanterns, shotguns, cider and bread. The men fired their guns through the branches, to encourage the good spirits to quell the bad, singing a song exhorting the tree to its best efforts, such as:

Bear blue, apples and pears enow
Barnsfull, bagsfull, sacksfull,
Hurrah!

and thrust a cider-soaked crust into the branches 'for the robin', a euphemism for the tree spirit. Today the procedure, if done at all, is done lightheartedly 'for luck'. It was once a serious magical rite. The ritual survives at Carhampton, near Minehead, Somerset, and until recent years also took place at Yakima, Washington State, some of whose founding apple stocks were brought from Carhampton round Cape Horn about 1820.

In the Ozarks region of the USA and the Tirol (Austria) apple trees were beaten to make them bear fruit. At Hildesheim, Germany, on New Year's Day people danced and sang round the trees

Wassailing the apple trees. (Above) Wassailers at Carhampton, Somerset, fire their guns into the apple trees on Twelfth Night. (Brian Shuel.) (Below) At Yakima, Washington State, USA, the bread is about to be dipped into the cider and the gun is ready. (Yakima Chamber of Commerce.)

to stimulate the crop. Ashes from the Yule log pushed among the branches increased the yield. German peasants tied their trees together and pronounced them 'married'. A rope of straw in which the Christmas sausages had rested was particularly effective. Romanians carried the dough of their *Turte* cake to their favourite tree; the husband playfully reproved the tree, threatening to fell it for poor performance, but his wife interceded: 'The tree will be as full of fruit as my hands are of dough.' The tree was warned — and spared to mend its ways.

Charities and 'Thomassing'

In England St Thomas's Day, 21st December ('Saint Thomas Grey, Saint Thomas Grey, longest night and shortest day'), the winter solstice, was the traditional day for the distribution of charities and doles. Then the poor visited the farmers 'corning', 'Thomassing' or 'gooding', collecting flour for Christmas baking. Donors received a 'lucky' holly sprig.

The kind-hearted remembered the less fortunate in their wills. John Popple of Burnham, Buckinghamshire, for example, left £40 a year in 1830 for ale, tobacco and snuff at the workhouse on Christmas Day.

The poor were not forgotten at Christmas. Here, on St Thomas's Day, 21st December, money is disbursed to the needy in the parish church.

At Piddlehinton, Dorset, the rector provided a pound of bread, a pint of Christmas ale and a mince pie to every poor applicant. In 1842 three hundred received the dole. Happily such disbursements have faded with greater affluence but fixed distributions may still occur on the traditional date. At Old Bolingbroke, Lincolnshire, grazing on 'Poor Folks Close' is let annually by candle auction and the proceeds are given to the poor on St Thomas's Day.

St Thomas's Day was also one of infant anarchy, when teachers were barred from schoolhouses until they provided treats. Parents might be similarly teased and servants daringly locked out their masters — a plain echo of Saturnalian frolics.

St Thomas's Night shares the supernatural quality of the season. In Austria it was a *Rauchnacht* ('smoke night'), when farms, barns and houses were purified with burning incense and holy water. Girls who slept with onions beneath their pillows on this auspicious night would have visions of their future husbands.

The Yule log

The Yule log, redolent of fragrant northern forests, travelled with Scandinavian invaders who kindled great solstitial fires as sun fortifiers and honourers of dark gods. In feudal England, the age of huge and hungry fireplaces, the log, snapping and crackling on a broad hearth, became the most popular expression of Christmas-tide. Of seasoned oak for preference ('for strength in the master and safety from thunder'), it was decorated with ribbons and dragged home in triumph from the woods on Christmas Eve. Anyone meeting the procession doffed his hat; it was a sight full of good omens. Over it the wassail bowl, drunk to the destruction of quarrels, bubbled merrily.

In Tuscany the whole festival is *Festa di Ceppo* (Festival of the Log). The German *Christbrand* or *Christklotz*, kindled on Christmas Eve, became a potent lightning charm. The common rule that the log must, at all costs, be kept burning through the Christmas Twelve Days recalled the primitive belief in the efficacy of perpetual fire. If the fire accidentally went out the omens were dire. On the plantations of the American South, Christmas lasted as long as the log burned, a custom brought, it was said, by farm emigrants from the north of England who expected ale and cider with meals while the log was alight. The slaves not unnaturally sought the wettest and greenest log they could find.

Before sunrise Serbians and Croatians felled two or three young oaks for each household, to the woodcutters' festive shout of 'Good Morning, Christmas!', and dragged them home, decorated with streamers and flowers, past lighted candles. The log was laid on the hearth with corn, an orange and a ploughshare, as offerings to ensure the farm's good health. Newfoundlanders cheerfully greeted the log's lighting at sunset on Christmas Eve with a fusillade from sealguns at every door. In the south of France the *souche de Noël* ('Christmas stump') was collected by the whole family, invoking a blessing. The youngest child anointed the log in the name of the Holy Trinity. Fragments provided charms and remedies; charcoal mixed with seedcorn improved the crop or saved the house from lightning and the family from chilblains; fruit trees, animals and poultry were cleared of vermin. A fragment built into Périgordian plough handles secured good germination or, if it were dropped in the well, kept the water sweet. Swedish households arranged the family silver on the Christmas table where the light from the log struck it, bringing good luck and, by reflective magic, an enhancement of wealth.

The Yule log still burns brightly at the Empress Hotel, Victoria, British Columbia, where, watched by guests from all over North America, it is proclaimed, sprinkled with wine and oil, dressed with wild boar's bristles for luck and, in proper style, fired with a cinder saved from last year's log (said to be kept under a hotel bed as a fire charm). The proclamation, 'with jester and seneschal,

Bringing the Yule log into the Great Hall on Christmas Eve.

17

with song and masque, with ceremony, pageantry and much rejoicing', is in accord with Robert Herrick's instructions of 1648:

> With the last year's brand,
> Light the new block, and
> For good success in his spending
> On your psaltries play
> That sweet luck may
> Come while the log is a-tending.

Even today it is possible to imagine the Yule log's dramatic entry into the house. As late as the 1880s Shropshire people could recall seeing it jingling home through the winter woods. Vessons Farmhouse, near the Stiperstones, showed a kitchen flagstone floor rutted and chipped by the iron-clad hooves of the carthorses which had hauled the log to the hearth.

The Ashen Faggot

Once universal in the farms and inns of Devon and Somerset, the Ashen Faggot, in some ways resembling the Yule log, still occasionally burns in some bar parlours. Ash is a significant tree, always associated with witchcraft and divination. Christians had another reason for revering it, believing that the Holy Child was bathed beside an ash-wood fire. The faggot of ash twigs, bound with nine withies of green ash (preferably all from one tree) and

Cutting the Ashen Faggot. Nine withies or ties were bound round the faggot. A jug of cider was drunk as each burned through.

Cutting sprays of the Glastonbury Thorn, Somerset, for the royal table. The tree is said to bloom on Christmas Day; in a suitable year this may indeed occur. (Norman Heal.)

drawn to the house by an obligatory four oxen, although one alone could easily have done the work, was, like the Yule Log, lighted with charcoal from last year's faggot. Unmarried girls each chose a withy; she whose band burst first would be first to marry. While the faggot roared and cracked like gunshots on the hearth and the handbells chimed, rank was forgotten and cider flowed. At the Luttrell Arms, Dunster, Somerset, the faggot is still lighted on Christmas Eve and, as custom dictates, a round of cider is served at the loss of every withy.

The Glastonbury Thorn

Every year the mayor and vicar of Glastonbury, Somerset, cut sprays from the Glastonbury Thorn for Queen Elizabeth II's Christmas table. St Joseph of Arimathea reputedly visited Glastonbury soon after the Crucifixion and planted his staff on the hill, where it rooted and flowered on Christmas Day. In 1753 the calendar changes caused predictable difficulties. *The Gentleman's Magazine* observed:

> '... a vast concourse of people attended the noted thorns on Christmas Day New-Stile, but to their great disappointment there was no appearance of its blowing, which made them watch it narrowly on the 6th January, the Christmas-Day, Old Stile, when it blowed as usual ...'

Of another Holy Thorn (perhaps a descendant) at Orcop, Herefordshire, a *Times* correspondent wrote in 1949 that he had watched the buds open to full flower within minutes of midnight on Old Christmas Eve. Botanically the thorn is *Crataegus monogyna 'biflora'*, which blooms in both winter and spring, although much depends on the weather.

The Haxey Hood Game

Old Christmas Day at Haxey, Humberside, has long been enlivened by a very ancient and complicated custom. In brief, Lady Mowbray, riding near Haxey in the thirteenth century, lost her scarlet hood in a stiff breeze. Twelve labourers gallantly retrieved it and were rewarded with lands to be played for annually by twelve 'boggans' dressed in red, the colour of the hood. A fool, face blackened, accompanies the 'king boggan'. He mounts a stone to announce the rules, referring mysteriously to the slaughter of bullocks. Meanwhile a fire of straw is lighted and the fool is 'smoked'. The game begins and players try to carry off 'hoods' (of rolled canvas) to their inns. In the late afternoon the 'sway' (the last hood, of leather) goes into play, a general mêlée follows, the 'sway' is captured and carried to the inn, where it hangs in the

The Haxey Hood Game: Rob Jarred throws the hood. (The Lincolnshire Standard Newspaper Group; Peter Row.)

winner's bar for the year to come. The local legend makes a pleasant story but folklorists believe that the game is the survival of a pre-Christian midwinter fertility ritual with animal sacrifice.

Tolling the Devil's Knell

The Devil's Knell or Old Lad's Passing Bell has tolled at Dewsbury, West Yorkshire, on Christmas Eve for over seven hundred years to celebrate the Devil's departure from the earth (and perhaps more specifically from Dewsbury) following the birth of Christ. Counting is precise. In December 1991 the tenor bell, known as Black Tom, was tolled exactly 1991 times and every year a stroke is added to the knell.

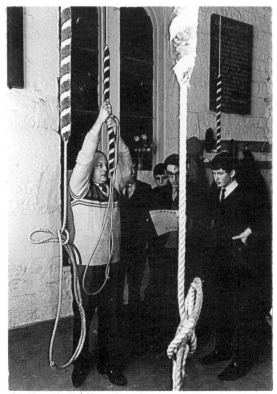

Tolling the 'Devil's Knell' at Dewsbury, West Yorkshire, on Christmas Eve. (Brian Shuel.)

3

CHRISTMAS FOLKLORE AND SUPERSTITION

Christmas Eve: a night of mystery

Christmas Eve, although hallowed for Christians, retains strong pagan associations. In 1891 Jerome K. Jerome, the novelist, noticing a marked appetite for fireside ghost stories among those gathering for Christmas, attributed this to the 'close, muggy atmosphere of Christmas that draws up ghosts, like the dampness that brings out frogs and snails'. It was probably a residue of the ancient concept of the dead's interest in the living on Christmas Eve.

Pious anticipation prevails in south and central Europe, in Scandinavia a consciousness of the supernatural qualities of these hours. No one with choice leaves the house that night, especially between cockcrow and daybreak. He may meet uncanny beings, such as trolls dancing or riding wolves. The dead revisit their former homes. A Swedish family cleans, polishes and tidies the parlour, leaving a fire for the revenants and the comforts of candles, food and Yule ale on the table. Traces of earth found on chairs next day settle the matter: the dead *have* called. Often the very word 'dead' is taboo; visitors were far more safely designated 'trolls'. It is worth taking trouble; a civil reception of the visitors brings good luck. So does an unlocked front door. But a few precautions never came amiss either: a cross in tar, fire or straw on the stable or a smear of Yule candle grease on the cows' udders was a useful aid in controlling the powers of darkness.

Christmas is still commonly welcomed by loud and cheerful noise such as bellringing, designated celebratory but once a protective noise. Austrians enjoy *Turmblasen* — loud music from brass instruments stationed on church towers on Christmas Eve. In the Swiss Valais bellringing contests are held between neighbouring Alpine valleys. Americans of the southern states fired shotguns and lighted fireworks — said to be a greeting for distant neighbours but more probably an updating of an old protective ritual.

A flourishing leisure skiing industry has given new emphasis to Christmas lights. There are torchlight processions and masked downhill races in Europe. At Sun Valley, Idaho, Dollar Mountain is fretted with fast-moving lights as the ski instructors race down it carrying lighted torches, as they also do at Jackson, Wyoming, and Bridger Bowl, Montana. The brilliance of the lights and the masks worn place these events well within the boundaries of the old protective custom of Christmas.

To welcome Christmas, a peal of bells is rung at Bow Church, London, in 1850. A scene in the ringing chamber.

Letting Christmas in

With the words 'Welcome old Father Christmas!' in Sussex it was lucky to be the one to fling open the front door at midnight on Christmas Eve. At the stroke of twelve Hanoverian front and back doors were opened 'to let the good in and the bad out'. Letting Christmas in was almost as important as letting in the New Year. The 'lucky bird' who did the deed, passing through every room in the house with a spring of evergreen in his hand, was rewarded in Lancashire by a welcoming penny left by the fire.

Christmas crops and weather

Fruit-growers from Illinois to Kent and Germany believe that snow at Christmas benefits their crop. Sun on North Carolina branches on Old Christmas Day augurs well. Snow during Christmas night or *Heiligerabend* bestows a special blessing on fruit to come. German peasants considered that the whole year's weather was 'made' during the Twelve Days and read weather signs for the months ahead accordingly. 'Christmas on the balcony, Easter by the fire' is the French view. That nothing sown on Christmas Eve will die, even if sown in snow, is the Dutch belief.

A pot of wheat and lentils sown on Sainte-Barbe's day (4th December) is a popular Provençal charm. If the seeds sprout by Christmas the gardener's luck for the year is assured. Ready-planted green-sprouting pots can be bought at every flower stall in Marseilles. This acceleration does not appear to diminish the magic!

24

The beasts kneel

The cattle in the byres joined in acknowledging Christmas by turning to the east at midnight in imitation of the beasts at Bethlehem. Some believed that they could also speak on this night and would bellow their adoration. In Herefordshire only seven-year-old beasts (the age of those in the stable) would kneel. Cattle of conservative tastes favoured Old Christmas Eve for all these activities (5th January), helping to confirm the superiority of the old calendar.

Sceptics were inevitable. One Ozarks man closely watched his father's oxen but his father insisted that a human observer broke the spell. Guernsey farmers provided extra hay but never dared to loiter to see it eaten. One did test his courage but the beasts cowshed door slammed shut, he dropped dead and no one repeated the experiment. A Nova Scotia farmer heard his cattle say: 'Tomorrow we'll be drawing wood to make our master's coffin.' The shocked farmer dropped dead on the spot, and as late as 1928 no one on this farm went near the cattle on Christmas Eve. They were fed in the afternoon.

Masked Trommelweiber at Ausseer, Austria, making a cheerful noise. They are traditional figures in Austrian Christmas processions. (Austrian National Tourist Office ö F V W/Herzberger.)

Bees, too, were involved in the mysteries. In Missouri they hummed the Old Hundredth Psalm or sang a carol at midnight. Several hives set together sent a satisfying volume of praise booming far across the garden. In Sussex, where bees were much respected, they were wassailed like the apple trees.

Extra rations

Everywhere the household's animals and birds received extra food at Christmas. In England beasts had hay, not straw. Norwegian cows still receive a special snack, 'as they were in the stable'. Salted herring is much to their taste. Denmark, Norway and Sweden remember wild birds with an unthreshed sheaf of wheat saved from harvest and nailed to a cartwheel on a pole or tied to the barn. Swedish farmers added a portion of every dish on the family table and ale for the horses. Silesian farmers carried a pocketful of corn throughout Christmas, then fed it to their hens to make them into good layers. Old customs continue: a group of fourteen mallard ducks on a pond at Walmer, Kent, received their Christmas 'sheaf' in 1991 in the thoroughly up-to-date form of a loaf of sunflower-seed bread.

Some beliefs have transferred themselves from farm animals to pets. (Two out of three dogs get presents, but fewer cats.) Dogs' Christmas stockings are commonplace; almost every standard pet treat can be found gift-wrapped. A dogs' Christmas cake filled with sausages, rusk, semolina and collagen and covered with real icing is produced; a Christmas dinner shaped into turkey legs and chips is planned.

Christmas superstitions

On Somerset farms Old Christmas Day was the beasts' holiday. Bad luck followed if horses were worked then. A farmer's wife harnessed her pony to take ducks to market; the pony shied on the way and she broke her leg.

Its grain eaten, the Yule sheaf had other uses. In Norway straws from it were thrown to the ceiling by the master of the house. As many as lodged in the rafters would there be sheaves at harvest. Prussians permitted no washing of clothes between Christmas and New Year; this was disrespectful to 'visitors'. Sweden banned fishing although nets might be set for luck.

Bread baked at Christmas and powdered was a useful remedy for dysentery and a healing portion for man and beast, even useful when pushed under the roots of orchard trees. Crumbled, it would extinguish a fire. Sussex cooks saw that a wisp of hay lay in the corner of the kitchen during Christmas baking; it must not be moved until Christmas had passed or luck would be thrown away.

A girl baking a 'dumb cake' on Christmas Eve. (From a drawing by H. Corbould, engraved by Finden.)

Exploiting the reputation of Christmas as a time for divination, a girl baked a 'dumb cake' (so named because it is made in silence) and, fasting on Christmas Eve, pricked it with her initials and left it on the hearthstone. At midnight her future husband would enter, through a door left open for him. A Christmas-born child would never be drowned or hanged. Some would acquire the gift of speech with animals. Dying during the season was advantageous: in Ireland they said that over the Twelve Days the gates of Heaven stood open.

4
THE CHRISTMAS FEAST

Christmas feasts may differ in detail but the emotions that inspire them are extraordinarily consistent. To forgather at the darkest point of the winter, to enjoy a great feast, the best fare available, ensures by sympathetic magic plenty in the year to come. Bonds with family and friends are strengthened in the home and, today, equally at the office party, the pub gathering and club dance. Lights blaze; greenery is mandatory. The ancient pagans would feel quite at home.

Holiday food has a character all its own. Christmas and New Year are marked by the making of thousands of distinctive cakes and biscuits. Many countries have a hundred to show. The profusion reflects early veneration of the corn spirit. Flour-rich biscuits shaped like animals or animal horns earlier assured the farm's fertility. Wheel-shaped sun-symbol cakes into which a candle could be set encouraged the sun's return.

Tradition binds the peoples of northern Europe — Denmark, parts of Germany, Finland, Norway and Sweden — who, with minor variations, serve *Julgröt*, porridge or rice pudding containing a single almond. Whoever finds the nut will variously be lucky, be first to marry or win a small prize (in Denmark often a marzipan pig). Inclusion of so plain a course in an exotic feast points to a memory of pre-Christian solstitial sacrifices to harvest gods.

Catholic countries count the Vigil of Christmas as a fast day. There, and in Scandinavia, fish is the principal item of the Christmas Eve meal. Stewed eels, carp or herring salad or dried cod (*Lutfisk*) are likely to be served.

In the Austrian Tirol *Zelten* or pie of dried fruits is ceremoniously baked on St Thomas's Eve. The *Zelten* is filled, sprinkled with holy water, marked with a cross before baking and then laid up in the rye store until Epiphany, when its cutting is a solemn affair. When an Austrian family leaves for Midnight Mass they leave milk on the table for the Virgin and Child.

Belgium has a bewildering array of festival biscuits. French Flanders famously has *coignoles* — oblong cakes with the Divine Child's image in sugar. On New Year's Day around Liège the famous Belgian waffles are made. The first, marked with a cross, is set on the mantelpiece as a gift for the crucifix. Once blessed, it will not rot and a small piece cures ills of man or beast. Like many others, Belgians invest special qualities in breads baked at Christmas.

Czechoslovakian delicacies are found wherever Czechs have settled. The round yeast bread *kolache* or *kolage* is often found in New York bakeries. It may have a succulent prune or poppy-seed filling and be ring-shaped with depressions for candles. The first is lighted on Christmas Eve, the second on Christmas Day and the third at the New Year. The cake is cut at Epiphany, when the family receives slices for luck. Once the cake was made early on Christmas morning with great ritual and divided by the father of the family. Baked stuffed carp with a rich sauce is a staple of the Czech feast. A chair is still left vacant at the Christmas table lest Christ call.

In Denmark the sociable feast begins on Christmas Eve with the almond porridge ritual. A sustaining meal of roast pork, duck with apple and prune stuffing, turkey, candied potatoes, red cabbage and jelly follows and on Christmas Day a great cold buffet of pickled herring, caviar, shrimps, meat balls, pâté, smoked leg of lamb, brawn, cold roast pork, smoked sausages and cheeses, topped with schnaps and beer. Guests may be at table from noon until late evening. On 26th December the ritual is repeated.

In Sweden the pig-shaped 'Yule boar loaf' holds the place of honour on the table through the holiday. An object linked with Freyr and harvest, it was once broken up and mixed with seedcorn

A Christmas Eve party in a West Country farmhouse with dancing, and a Kissing Bunch well used. Cider flows freely.

or given to the plough team to eat to link the seasons by linear magic.

The French feast — *le réveillon* (or midnight revel) — takes place after mass on Christmas Eve, with oysters, champagne and *bûche de Noël* — the famous log-shaped French Christmas cake with cream filling and chocolate icing with a tree-bark pattern. Feast details vary with region: in Alsace goose takes place of honour; in Burgundy, turkey and chestnuts; Paris and the Île de France favour oysters and *bûche*.

In Provence, for the most important meal of Christmas, the *gros souper* (great supper) eaten on Christmas Eve, three tablecloths rest on the table. Formerly these stayed in place for weeks, the first removed for the Feast of the Circumcision, the second for Pentecost. Three candles still burn for the Trinity and twelve rolls on the table represent the Apostles, and a larger loaf Christ. As the last meal of Advent the *gros souper* is *maigre* or meatless. Grey mullet with olives, salt cod, snails, pasta and eggs are served, followed by the traditional thirteen desserts of southern France. These might include nuts still in their shells, tangerines, dried figs, dates and apricots, melon, apples and nougat, a rich bread called *pompe à l'huile* and *fougasse*, a bread in lattice shape. The desserts, recalling by number Christ and his Apostles, were presented with pride by careful housewives as a sign of prosperity and good housekeeping.

There were links with more distant, darker gods. In Berry the Christmas loaves distributed to the poor were *cornaboeux* and crescent-shaped. In Lorraine people gave *cognés*, two pastry crescents back to back. These horn-shaped cakes were perhaps substitutes for earlier sacrifices of live oxen. Near Chartres *cochenilles* and *coquelin* in animal and human shapes were popular and *naulets*, doll-like figures of the Holy Child, were seen in bakers' baskets.

Finland's feasting begins on Christmas Eve after church with roast pork, ham wrapped in rye dough and carrot pudding. Germany abounds in carp ponds and the dish at both Christmas and New Year feasts is carp in red wine or beer. Roast goose is also popular. A final delicacy is *Rumtopf* or 'rumpot': summer fruits — strawberries, cherries, raspberries, pears and peaches — are packed into jars and marinated in rum until Christmas, when the pot is broached and the fruit eaten with cream as dessert.

Germany's favourite Christmas cake is *Dresdner Christstollen*, a tunnel loaf of flour, butter, almonds, marzipan, fruit and nuts, weighing about 5 pounds (2.3 kg). Every German family has one, made to a recipe known from the fourteenth century. The most delicious *Stollen* are said to be those baked in Dresden.

Another fruit bread is Swabian *Hutzelbrot* (dried fruit bread), one of the traditional offerings at Nuremberg's *Christkindlesmarkt*. The Christmas tree came from Germany; appropriately, the country also has the *Baumkuchen*, the Berlin tree-cake, resembling a tree trunk. Spiced biscuit dough is poured over a turning spit and each layer is glazed with sugar as it forms. The finished cake may be as much as 6 feet (1.8 metres) long and is served in finely shaved slices.

Lebkuchen, spiced honey cakes in shapes of people, houses, hearts and animals, are particularly associated with Nuremberg, where, around Christmas, E. O. Schmidt, Germany's largest *Lebkuchen* factory, on the outskirts of the city, is reported to make 1½ million *Lebkuchen* daily in five shapes and to ten recipes. Star shapes are made only at Christmastide. Some mothers still bake honeycake houses for their children on Christmas Eve.

Home biscuit-making is popular in German homes from the start of Advent. Housewives may make 25 different types, iced, coloured and flavoured with ginger, nutmeg, anise, cardamom and vanilla, from Aachen's *Printen*, rectangular and spicy, to Rhineland's *Spekulatius* (*Springerle* in southern Germany), and *Pfeffernüsse* gingernuts and *Zimtsterne* cinnamon stars. *Spekulatius* pastry is pressed into moulds carved with animal motifs and religious and Christmas scenes. A pile of holiday biscuits, nuts and marzipan at each place is an important part of the Christmas Eve feast and biscuits also fill the children's shoes on St Nicholas's Day.

Richard Blakeborough's account of Christmas on his Yorkshire farm in 1898 tells of British rituals which have faded only within living memory:

> Our greatest observance of custom is, as it should be, in connexion with Christmas-tide. Indeed, preparation for the same really commences some weeks in advance. There is the pudding to make and partly boil; all the ingredients for the plum-cake to order; the mincemeat to prepare for the mince-pies; the goose to choose from some neighbouring farmer's stock; the cheese to buy; and the wheat to have hullins beaten out and to cree [stew], for the all-important frumenty; the Yule-cake or pepper-cake to make; the hollin to gather ...

Frumenty, stewed or creed wheat, was eaten with new milk, sugar and nutmeg first thing in the morning, denoting ritual origins. The ubiquitous almond porridge of Europe and the magical snack of *rommegröt* vital to the good temper of *Tomte* and *Nisse* share these associations with harvest spirits. Once frumenty had

Farmer Giles, his family and servants sit down to Christmas dinner in 1800, at one end of the table an enormous Christmas pudding, at the other a baron of beef. An etching by A. W. Heath published in 1830.

been finished at Christmas no more was made until the next year.

In Britain rich Christmas cakes have always been popular. A late Victorian recipe required flour, sugar, butter, eggs, peel, blanched almonds, cherries, raisins, sultanas, brandy or rum. The Yule Dough or Yule Baby of pastry or gingerbread, with currants marking eyes, mouths and coat buttons, was presented by bakers to their customers, recalling less a pre-Reformation Holy Child than a sacrificial victim. Yule cake, a Yorkshire delicacy of flour, yeast, raisins, currants, lemon peel and nutmeg, was eaten on Christmas Eve. Large as a dinner plate, 3 inches (75 mm) thick, decorated with a lattice of pastry, and still surviving, particularly in North Yorkshire, is the pungent gingerbread peppercake, served with Wensleydale cheese (into which a cross had been cut with a knife point). To the south-west in Shropshire 'wigs' — caraway seed buns — dipped in mulled ale and eaten on Christmas Eve, were a tradition. No one attempted to count the loaves of Scottish Yule bread ritually baked in silence, lest ill-luck descend.

Another English speciality, the Christmas pie, with a filling of beef, suet, sugar, currants, raisins, lemons, spices, orange peel, goose, tongue, fowls and eggs (a recipe of 1822), and in a nineteenth-century Sussex version apples and brandy too, was the ancestor of the mince pie, central to the English Christmas. Nottinghamshire children about 1850 were given 'mince pigs', with long snouts, curling tails and crimped backs. Before the Reformation mince pies were oval, cradle-shaped, with a pastry image of the Holy Child in swaddling bands. In the 1650s Puritans objected to such 'idolatry'. The pies vanished. With the Restoration of the Monarchy in 1660 they came back but now they were non-Catholic, smaller, round and sweet. In England the religious connection had disappeared; the pies were now sweet desserts and never again savouries.

It is unlucky to refuse the offer of a mince pie, seen as a token rejection of seasonal luck. To eat a pie on each of the Twelve Days ensures twelve happy months; but the pies must be offered by a friend and baked in dozens to strengthen the charm. Today the mince pie is more popular than ever, attempted (using ready-made mincemeat and pastry) by many novice cooks and sold in thousands by supermarkets, grocers and bakers in several continents. The present mixture, raisins, sultanas, currants, peel, apples, almonds, suet, molasses, sugar and brandy, is only tenuously linked with the Christmas pie, whose filling had thirteen ingredients for Christ and his Apostles and always a little chopped mutton 'in remembrance of the shepherds'.

Christmas feasts often show their origins. Countries of the old British Empire — Australia, Canada, New Zealand and South Africa — still share British traditions. About 1865 Lady Barker, on her pioneer New Zealand sheep station, gave a Christmas party for her shepherds and shearers. Their host tempted them, shy Scots, to the party with loans of 'tidy clothes' while Lady Barker, a novice cook, feverishly studied her recipes. Kind neighbours sent fruit, vegetables and geese and her husband rode 20 miles (32 km) for a sirloin of beef. (It was a point of honour never to serve mutton, except disguised as curry.) Leaves and ferns gathered at dawn decorated the wash-house; carpenters disguised the copper with flags to hold the dessert. The words of the Christmas service were said (Lady Barker reflected that it was the very first time that these sacred words had been heard in the valley). Although it was a sultry day, with no breath of air, the big musical box was wound up, the guests were shown to the tables and their hostess noticed with satisfaction that 'they ate incessantly for two hours'.

The Greeks bake *Christpsomo*, 'Christ's bread', marked with the sign of the cross and eaten when the family returns from mass at four o'clock on Christmas morning. Everything is left ready overnight for the arrival of Christ, including this loaf. There are no presents or Christmas tree; these wait for St Basil's Day (1st January). Several courses of the Greek Christmas meal are blessed in church before they are eaten. Pork is a staple. Country housewives also bake special buns for cattle and hens. One bun, dedicated to the land, is nailed up as a charm and the cattle buns are crumbled and salted and given to cows for luck.

Italian *panettone*, a tender sweet bread with raisins and candied citron, baked in a round and marked with a cross, is popular at all festivals. Legend tells of a young nobleman who fell in love with the pretty daughter of a Milan baker. To gain her favour, he took a job in the bakehouse, invented *panettone* and so delighted the baker that he immediately agreed to the match. Equally popular are *amaretti* (macaroons) and a nougat (*torrone*), survivors of the sweet dishes once enjoyed at Kalends. The Italian *cenone*, or 'great feast', on Christmas Eve includes stewed eels.

The Dutch cherish ancient traditions. The big day for children is 6th December, St Nicholas's Day, *Sinterklaas*, when they are given biscuits shaped like their own initials. Adults receive *banketletter*, a pastry filled with almond paste topped with glacé cherries and shaped like the family initials. *Banketletter* comes in all shapes and sizes, plain, milk, white or pastel chocolate, marzipan, praline or nougat-filled, from stocking stuffers to larger examples with roses, ribbons and foil filigree decorations.

Speculaas, a spiced gingerbread cookie shaped like windmills, bishops and houses (for heartier appetites is the *speculaas brokje*, 'speculaas brick' — the same width and length as one of the old paving stones), *pepernote*, a small round, spicy biscuit, and *gevulde speculaas*, a softer version filled with marzipan, are other favourites. Accompanying all Christmas meals is *Kerstbrood* (raisin loaf stuffed with marzipan).

Western Norway has *Lutfisk*, sun-dried, lye-cured and jelly-like cod, served with white sauce; lamb, wind-dried and salted, smoked as in Viking times (enjoyed in Iceland as *hangikjót*); and fresh and marinated salmon on a bed of birch twigs. The inevitable *Julgröt* appears. In eastern Norway side-roast pork is the choice, washed down with caraway-flavoured *Linje aquavit*. This has been matured in casks on ships which must cross the Equator twice before returning the liqueur to Scandinavia. Each bottle bears the name of the ship that carried it.

From early December Norwegian hotels and restaurants advertise Christmas feasts — *Julebord* — in the Oslo papers. People travel from as far away as Denmark to attend. Down the length of long dining-room tables are displayed every variant of *hors d'oeuvres*, meat, fowl, fish, fruit, dessert and cheese. For an all-in single price the diner can eat as much, as long, and as adventurously as he likes from six until midnight, choosing from a whole lobster, roast beef, oysters, cold roast reindeer, pork stuffed with prunes and apples, smoked sausages, herring or the essential pig ribs. If able, he may dance between courses.

Poles, devout Catholics, send their friends blessed *oplatki* wafers as Christmas cards. When the first star appears on Christmas Eve the family ritually break a wafer among themselves while exchanging good wishes. During the afternoon of Christmas Eve a great silence falls over Polish towns; shops close; everyone is at home preparing the feast. In every window candles welcome the Holy Family. The tablecloth is laid over a layer of hay commemorating the manger. In some parts a wheatsheaf stands in each corner of the room. The sheaves are later taken to the orchard as a fruit charm and a feast for the birds.

Romanian *turte*, a pastry of many paper-thin layers with sugar, honey and walnut, eaten on Christmas Eve, has a plaited finish resembling the Holy Child's swaddling clothes. On *Natal a Portugesa*, 6th January, the Portuguese enjoy *Bolo de Rei*, Three Kings' Cake, a sweet bread with garnishes of pineapple, cherries and walnuts, representing the jewels of the Kings' crowns.

Sweden's famous Boar Loaf is on the table through the holiday. Breads, cardamom-flavoured and coloured with saffron; the traditional gingerbread figures of Nissel and Nasse; and biscuits shaped like Thor's sacred goat and the sunwheel make up the 'Yule Pile' of biscuits by every plate on Christmas morning.

Among Swiss baked goods, the Zürich *Tirggel*, derived from the

A 'Tirggel' or Christmas pastry, of flour, sugar and honey, from Canton Zurich, Switzerland. It is shaped in an old carved mould before baking. (Swiss National Tourist Office/Switzerland.)

flat Germanic pagan sacrificial cake, originally bore animal images. The dough is pressed into wooden moulds, many of historical interest in their own right. Animals have been joined by pictures of the Christmas story and of such heroes as William Tell. The *Tirggel* keeps its place under the Christmas tree.

The traditional Christmas cake, rich, lushly fruited, glowing and gleaming with glacé fruits, toasted nuts and sometimes finished with marzipan and frosting and decorations such as robins, holly sprigs, Santa Clauses and reindeer, is today found in its most exotic form in the United States. Such cakes have in the twentieth century become favourite offerings from businesses to clients. Once again they express imitative magic. To partake of such a cake, even at arm's length, ensures plenty for the year to come and by inference business prosperity on both sides. From late autumn onwards the business newspapers carry lyrical advertisements by cake purveyors.

In addition to cakes, the United States enjoys a huge variety of national dishes, cakes and biscuits using recipes originally brought to North America by immigrants. Nearly every delicacy mentioned elsewhere in this chapter is available in America. Particularly influential were the Moravians of Pennsylvania. Their womenfolk began making *kummelbrod*, mince-pies and biscuits months before Christmas. Shapes used by the Moravians, such as animals, stars, Christmas trees, holly leaves, bells and angels, had a wide appeal and today these shapes are the mainstay of every cookie-cutter set sold in American supermarkets.

The boar's head

During Scandinavian Yule the chosen food was the boar's head, the food of Valhalla's heroes, eaten in honour of the Sun Boar and always the first dish to be placed on the table of the medieval great hall. Today, against all odds, it holds its own as an item of Christmas diet, playing several ancient roles, as a food, as a vehicle of ancient custom and as an object of magic. In the forests of Europe, including those of the Rhineland, Bavaria, Prussia and Luxembourg, the boar is still hunted. It often appears on menus.

At Queen's College, Oxford, the boar's head is carried into the college hall for the Christmas feast on a silver platter dated 1668, while the 'Boar's Head Carol' is sung:

> The Boar's Head in hand bear I
> Bedeck'd with bays and rosemary
> And I pray you, my masters, be merry
> *Quot estis in convivio,*
> *Caput apri defero,*
> *Reddens laudes Domino.*

The boar's head ready to be carried in the procession at Indiana University's Madrigal Feast. In the boar's teeth is a red apple, a sun symbol. (Indiana University.)

The singers receive the decorations from the boar's head, the orange from the teeth and the crown from the forehead. The dish would suit medieval appetites: in 1883 the Queen's College head weighed 65 pounds (29.5 kg).

Both the Norse gods of fertility, Freyr and Freyja, owned and rode boars; almost all Indo-European, Norse and Celtic peoples revered the beast. The head was protective. Swedish war gear (including a helmet in the seventh-century Sutton Hoo treasure) carried its motif, as *Beowulf* describes:

> Each helmet sparkled
> With its glancing boar-emblems; brilliants with gold,
> Patterned and fire-tempered, it guarded the life
> Of its brave battle-wearer.

Tradition holds that the boar cult came to England with Anglo-Saxon invaders and spread to the United States during the colonial period.

Indiana University, Bloomington, Indiana, has held a very successful and popular Boar's Head Ceremony as part of its annual Madrigal Feast for many years. So popular is the occasion that seven separate dinners are held to accommodate all those wishing to attend. The traditionally decorated boar's head is carried in

37

The decorated and beflagged boar's head from the ceremony at Queen's College, Oxford.

procession, accompanied by madrigal singers in Renaissance dress from the University's School of Music. Presided over by a Lord of Misrule, appropriately garbed, a sumptuous dinner, rich in tradition, follows, with fanfares, jugglers, wassailers, the wassail cup and plum pudding in the authentic atmosphere of Tudor England. The panelling and Gothic arches of Alumni Hall, where the Madrigal Feast takes place, make a most appropriate setting for the festivities.

Even modern Britain preserves faint echoes of pig sacrifices. Ham, brawn, stuffed pork chine and sausages are still served as accompaniments to the turkey. At Gurk, Carinthia, Austria, a pig killed on Christmas Eve was made into fresh sausages eaten at supper after Midnight Mass. People in Luxembourg enjoy pork, tripe and *gehauk*, a dish of pig's liver and heart, served on New Year's Eve. Families gather after Midnight Mass for jellied piglets, black puddings and sausages. In Natchez, Mississippi, a *cochon de lait* or sucking pig is important in the celebrations. In Hungary the typical New Year dish of roast sucking pig, crisp and golden, apple in mouth, surrounded with red cabbage and pickled gherkins, brings luck for the year. If a whole pig prove too much, diners acquire equal merit from tackling any pork dish.

German farmers saved the straw in which the Christmas sausages had rested and bound its magical garlands round fruit trees on Christmas Eve. The tree would oblige with a good crop. Pigs' entrails and bones, even the straw from their sties, had fertilising properties.

Roast beef, turkey and goose

The supreme 'roast beef of Old England' and venison were once supported by geese, capons, pheasants, bustards and swans at the feast. The peacock, always a spectacular bird, would be skinned, the plumage set aside intact, the bird roasted, sewn back into its plumage and presented at table with gilded beak and fanned tail.

The goose held sway until well into the nineteenth century but finally gave way to turkey, today's most popular Christmas dish in the English-speaking world. About 1519 the Spaniards had brought the bird (native to North and Central America) from Mexico to Spain, then to the Spanish Netherlands and finally to the English Fens. By 1542 it appeared regularly at English tables. East Anglia became its home and breeding ground. Farmers drove great flocks

Bakeries cooked the Christmas dinners of those whose homes lacked ovens, or whose ovens were not large enough to hold a joint or bird. The advertisement reads: 'Old Christmas Ale, 6d per pot'. A Leech drawing.

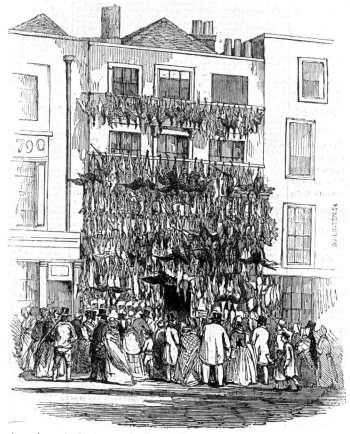

A poulterer's Christmas display, Holborn Hill, London, 1845. The wide variety of birds available is clearly seen.

of turkeys to London for the season, stopping to allow the birds to graze and rest at the roadside and taking weeks over the journey. As a latecomer the turkey has attracted little folklore, except that two people should each hold one end of a wishbone or 'merrythought' from a carcase, wish and pull. Whoever wins the larger piece gets his wish, provided he keeps it secret and remains silent throughout.

Households with small ovens were glad of the help of bakers in cooking the Christmas joint or bird. People would hurry to the baker's shop after morning service, carrying clean white cloths to throw over the freshly cooked meat — identified by a numbered skewer pushed into each joint as it went into the oven to ensure that everyone got his property back.

Christmas pudding

Plum porridge, an early favourite, went out of fashion in the late eighteenth century. It was a strange dish of beef and mutton broth with crumbs, raisins, currants, wine, spices and herbs, eaten with a spoon with the meat course. From this evolved the stiffer Christmas pudding, at first boiled in a pudding cloth (early puddings are recognisable by roundness; later they were confined to a basin). Ingredients remain constant; a classic pudding today might contain suet, brown sugar, raisins, currants, citron, lemon and orange peels, spices, crumbs, flour, eggs, milk and brandy. The pudding, unmistakably a dessert to the British, can cause confusion. A British guest presented her Norwegian hostess with a Christmas pudding and was amused to find it set out (logically enough) with the vegetables.

The Sunday nearest to St Andrew's Day (30th November) — 'Stir Up Sunday', from the collect for the day, 'Stir up, we beseech

Making the Christmas pudding.

41

Thee, O Lord, the wills of thy faithful people' — is traditional for pudding mixing. In the Royal Navy puddings are ritually stirred by cooks delving with paddles into flag-hung grog tubs. Custom requires that a distinguished visitor or the senior officer present stir first. Puddings must be stirred with wood (remembering the manger) and sunwise, to confirm the sun's course (or to copy, some say, the Magi's approach route). Everyone present stirs for luck. Three wishes go to each stirrer; only one is granted. Thirteen ingredients recall Christ and the Apostles. Some families make a thirteenth pudding, named 'Judas', to be given to a tramp, allowed to moulder or thrown away. Victorian households liked orderly stirring; father first, followed by all in the household down to the newest kitchen maid. Charms hidden in the pudding indicated the future: a ring, marriage; a button, batchelorhood; a thimble, an old maid; a sixpence, good luck. He who eats Christmas pudding in thirteen different houses before 1st January will experience exceptional joy. Brandy poured over the pudding is lighted and the flickering blue flames in a darkened room link modern diners in spirit with Norse forebears.

Drinks

Drinks flow freely. The first-footers' 'hot pint' launches the Scottish New Year. Lambswool, mainstay of wassail bowls, is a mixture of hot ale, roasted apples, sugar, nutmeg, ginger, eggs, cream and bread snippets. Devon 'egg-hot', cider heated with spices and eggs, has the bland eggnog of the American supermarkets as a pallid descendant. A nineteenth-century recipe is livelier; twelve egg yolks, a pint of brandy, a quart of cream, milk, sugar and spices, with whipped egg white as a snowy crown. In the far Shetland Isles they drank *whipcoll*, egg yolk beaten with sugar on which cream was slowly poured and the whole finished with rum or brandy. In homely style at Over, Cambridgeshire, the parish bellringers had their annual supper at the Swan Inn on New Year's Eve, with roast beef and a powerful 'hot pot', made by the landlord himself, of beer, spirits, eggs, sugar, nutmeg and milk, drunk from a cowhorn called Long Tot.

On the Isle of Man *Jough-y-Nollick* ('drink of Christmas') seems to owe its name to the Vikings who settled the island. There, brewing pans served the whole neighbourhood; to be active was 'to go about like a brewing pan'. A posset of hot milk, ale, sugar and spices, heated in a tin can with a red-hot poker, may still be found in old-fashioned pubs. Sloe gin, perry and hot elderberry wine are also popular. The University of Cambridge liked 'bishop', mulled port prepared with roasted lemons, all bristling with cloves like hedgehogs.

The wine is blessed at Greiveldange, Luxembourg, on 26th December. (Luxembourg Tourist Office.)

In north Germany *Grog*, a mixture of rum and hot water (a well known recipe suggests 'Rum is necessary and water may also be used'), in Europe *Glühwein*, mulled red wine with cinnamon and cloves, and in Sweden *Glögg*, mulled red wine with a hefty dash of aquavit, are drunk everywhere. The making of *Feuerzangenbowle* ('firetongs punch'), for the waiting hours of New Year's Eve, is a fire charm in its own right. Heated red wine with lemon rind, cloves, cinnamon and oranges is put into a copper pan, over a *réchaud* or hot plate. Above it a sugar-cone is set in a holder. Rum is poured over the cone and lighted and melting sugar drips into the wine. Rum is added until the cone is completely melted. Special *Feuerzangenbowle* sets are popular Christmas presents.

German brewers have always produced a strong *Weihnachtsbier* or 'Christmas ale'. Reckoned to be the strongest beer in the world is Swiss *Samichlaus* or 'Santa Claus', brewed in December and matured for a year before drinking.

Most Christmas drinking is unceremonious with toasts and good wishes in the spirit of the season. But at Greiveldange, Luxembourg, greater formality is enjoyed on 26th December, when vinegrowers parade with the local band and carry wine to church to be blessed. Afterwards the barrel is broached and there is a tasting for all present.

43

Putting up the evergreens at home on Christmas Eve, under Grandma's watchful eye, 1855.

Decorating the village church, 1860; from a drawing by J. Leech. Mistletoe is still generally banned from church decorations.

5

CHRISTMAS GARLANDS AND GREENERY

The Romans' evergreen decorations, life symbols in midwinter, sheltered vegetation spirits when other trees had lost their leaves. Christians wasted no time in blending these beliefs with their own concept of everlasting life.

In his *Survey of London* (1598) John Stow wrote that churches, houses, street standards and conduits 'were decked with holme, ivie, bayes and whatsoever the season of the yeare affordeth to be greene'. Not only on land have evergreens been displayed. The Royal Navy hoists evergreens to mastheads at Christmas and no Norwegian ship, anywhere in the world, is without its masthead Christmas tree, glowing with white lights, on Christmas Eve. Today the Swedes strew their entrance halls with evergreen twig tips and set a young spruce on either side of the front door.

Strict rules governing the use of evergreens point to former magical roles. To bring evergreens indoors before Christmas Eve was unlucky; to remove them before or keep them in place after Twelfth Night or, in removing the leaves, to let even one touch the ground was dangerous. Premature removal disposed of luck. However evergreens were removed, it must be a thorough job. Every leaf overlooked had its burden of ill-luck:

> Down with the rosemary and so
> Down with the baies and mistletoe,
> Down with the holly, ivie, all
> Wherewith you drest the Christmas hall.
> That so the superstitious find
> Not one least branch there left behind,
> For look, how many leaves there be,
> Neglected there, maids trust to me,
> So many goblins you shall see.

People sent their most reliable servants to sweep private pews at church lest a stray leaf or berry be overlooked.

The holly and the ivy

No plant has warmer associations with Christmas than holly (*Ilex aquifolium*). Handsome, shining, barbed leaves and scarlet berries, a symbol of eternal life, made it an important plant in Saturnalian decorations long before its adoption by the early Christians. Red protects against witchcraft; holly is still rejected as a decoration if it is berryless and sterile. Christmas lifts the normal taboo on cutting holly. Beliefs, other than those dealing with

A mistletoe seller, drawn by Phiz.

evergreens in general, rule its use. It must, as a male symbol, be brought in only by a man. A sprig nailed up in the cowshed made the beasts thrive and the berries were valued as a powerful animal medicine, doubly potent if the sprig came from church decorations (unlike mistletoe, holly is permitted in churches). A berried sprig is the proper adornment for the top of the Christmas pudding and a scrap is preserved and burned under next year's plum pudding, a charm of continuity. In a subservient capacity, ivy (*Hedera*), a kindly, clinging, feminine companion to holly, worked to secure the household's fertility.

Mistletoe

Mistletoe (*Viscum album*), the Golden Bough of legend, grows from the Baltic to the Mediterranean and everywhere enjoys a formidable reputation for magic. In Norse myth a mistletoe dart killed Baldur, the sun god. Cut with a golden knife at midnight on Christmas Eve, the plant figured in druidic magic and medicine. Its connection with lightning, storms and the northern sky gods is strong; the Swiss name is *Donnerbesen* — 'thunder besom'. It

46

grew neither on earth nor in heaven, men said, and therefore would preserve life. Chopping down a mistletoe-bearing tree was desecration. Pagan associations still bar it from churches (except for York Minster, where a general pardon was proclaimed until its removal on Twelfth Night). Its handler must see that it never touches the ground. A sprig fed to the first cow to calve after the New Year brought luck to the dairy. Kissing under the mistletoe may be the very last flicker of Saturnalian licence. Any girl unsaluted will not marry during the year to come. Ozarks farmers found practical benefit in mistletoe and put a bunch in their smokehouses 'to keep the witches off the meat'.

Poinsettia and rosemary

The poinsettia (*Euphorbia pulcherrima*), with its bright red bracts, now the accepted Christmas symbol of North America, turns up in every Christmas connection, on cards, wrapping paper, labels, seals, table linen and as a pot plant. It was discovered in Mexico in 1834 (its Mexican name is 'Flower of the Holy Night') and developed by Dr Joel R. Poinsette of South Carolina. The world's largest Christmas poinsettia display — over ten thousand are propagated for the Christmas Showing — is at Bellingrath Gardens, Theodore, Alabama. Poinsettias appear in many settings,

The 15 foot (4.5 metre) Christmas tree made of red and white poinsettias in the mall at Bellingrath Gardens, Theodore, Alabama. (Bellingrath Gardens.)

Phiz's drawing of Christmas Eve at Mr Wardle's, from 'The Pickwick Papers' by Charles Dickens.

as tree standards and in hanging baskets, as decorations for the Christmas table and, particularly impressively, in the shape of a 15 foot (4.6 metre) 'tree' of red and white poinsettias which reaches from the floor nearly to the ceiling.

Its soft blue flowers link the evergreen rosemary with the Virgin Mary. The shrub is said to grow upwards for 33 years until it is as tall as Christ, then to grow in width only. According to legend, it blooms at midnight on Old Christmas Eve.

The Kissing Bunch

The Kissing Bunch, precursor of the later arriving Christmas tree, for centuries reigned supreme during the Twelve Days in England and the United States. Made of two bisecting hoops, the Bunch was decorated with holly and ivy, ribbons, baubles, apples, oranges and nuts and sometimes, when all decorations were home-made, ivy berries glazed in flour or powdered glass. A mistletoe spray hung below, slowly revolving in the candles' draught. A trio of dolls, suggesting the Bunch's pre-Reformation origins, also hung from it, called 'Our Saviour', 'Mary' and 'Joseph'. Hoops were preserved from year to year and hung on hooks used for no other purpose. In Staffordshire the Bunch was hung about five o'clock on Christmas Eve, wrote one enthusiast, 'with many a romp and a kiss … and indeed for the next day or two, kissing was the sole order of things under this bunch, every visitor being kissed and having to kiss.'

In the Rhaetian Alps of Austria is *Sylvesterabend*, a New Year custom with some resemblance to the Kissing Bunch. People linger late in the inns, which are decorated with greenery. From the centre of the parlour ceiling hangs a wreath of pine twigs and in a corner 'Sylvester', old and ugly with a flaxen beard and mistletoe wreath, hides. If a youth or girl happens to pass under the wreath, Sylvester leaps out and claims a kiss. At midnight, as the repre-sentative of the old year, he is driven away.

The Christmas tree

The Christmas tree's story is obscure. One legend suggests that Martin Luther compared its twinkling candles with the starry heavens on the night of Christ's birth and introduced it to his people. It is known to have reached America before Britain.

The Christmas tree market, Covent Garden, London, about 1866.

George III's Hessian troops carried it there with them and found German settlers in Pennsylvania already familiar with the custom.

In England German merchants living near Manchester before 1840 are said to have decorated Christmas trees for their children and a children's party at Queen Caroline's court in 1821 set up boughs of evergreen in the German manner. In 1841 Queen Victoria, whose consort Prince Albert was German, had her first Christmas tree at Windsor Castle. In the Windsor dining-room in 1847 waited a baron of beef, a boar's head with rosemary and bays and Christmas trees on the sideboards, loaded with presents. Each trees was lighted with eighty wax candles. The popularisation of the Christmas tree through royal example never faltered. Charles Dickens may have referred to it as 'the new German toy' but it soon meant that the days of the old English Kissing Bunch were numbered.

The public tree

Probably the most famous Christmas tree in the world and part of any London Christmas is the tree given to the City of West-minster by the City of Oslo, Norway. The first tree was brought over in 1947 as a token of Norwegian appreciation of British friendship during the Second World War, when, after the German invasion, the Norwegian monarch and government moved to London for the duration.

The tree is a Norwegian spruce, some 70 feet (21 metres) high and about sixty years old. A cargo ship of the Fred Olsen Line brings the tree to Felixstowe free of charge, whence it is taken to its traditional site in Trafalgar Square. The lights are all white, following the effect of the earlier wax candles. At lighting-up time the National Gallery dims its floodlighting for maximum effect. At the crib nearby, arranged by the vicar of St Martin's-in-the-Fields church, carol singers meet from then every night until Christmas. Two other well-known trees stand in St Paul's Cathedral, both the gift of Queen Elizabeth II and from her Sandringham estates.

Another always elegant example of a public tree, 70 feet (21 metres) high with eighteen thousand multicoloured lights and 5 miles (8 km) of wire, stands in the Rockefeller Centre, New York City. Another, transformed with lights every Christmas, grows in the lawns of the British Columbia Parliament Buildings, Victoria, Canada. In Washington the National Christmas Tree of the United States is lighted up by the President himself. The world's tallest living Christmas tree, a 150 foot (46 metre) high Sitka spruce, is said to be in Ferndale, California.

Christmas trees bring out generosity. The little coast community

Above: *The Trafalgar Square Christmas tree, an annual gift from the city of Oslo, ready for transport to London. (Fred Olsen Agencies Ltd.)*

Below: *The tree at night.*

of Garibaldi, Oregon, knowing that Nevada cannot grow Christmas trees, sends to Reno and Sparks the gift of two 60 foot (18 metre) Douglas firs and even arranges that Santa Claus delivers them.

The family tree

In families it is the home Christmas tree that receives most attention. In Germany the mother of the family, working alone behind closed doors, decorates the tree with spun glass and tinsel globes (close relations of the sun symbols carried by the boar's head). *Rauschgoldengel*, spice cakes (often gilded), home-made biscuits (animals, stars and hearts), red apples, nuts, straw stars, *Engelshaar* (Angels' Hair), marzipan favours, tinsel garlands and beeswax candles make it an object of radiance and beauty. Nearby she prepares the *Weihnachtstisch* — 'Christmas table' — where the presents will be displayed.

In the Scandinavian countries and in Holland tree lights are white, a link with the former white beeswax candles still seen in Bavaria. Small national flags are the usual decoration. Swedish tree trimming is completed with little marzipan pigs (another link with the Sun-boar). The 'Christmas Tree Fairy' or 'Star' into which, in a less pious age, the earlier angel may have changed,

A lighted living tree stands in front of the Parliament Buildings, Victoria, British Columbia. (Province of British Columbia.)

Nuremberg Rauschgoldengel, the pleated gold foil angels which are almost a symbol of German Christmas itself. (Stadt Nürnberg.)

dances on the top of the tree. Tradition is jettisoned entirely at the Christmas gathering for cowboys at Cody, Wyoming: a Stetson hat tops the tree.

After the revolution in Russia, Santa Claus became Father Winter or Grandfather Frost. Christmas as such was not celebrated but some customs survived, such as the flag-decked Christmas tree which became the 'New Year Tree', linked with children's games.

Not until the technical advances of the 1870s did the glassblowers of Thuringia in eastern Germany discover how to decorate the insides of the fragile glass globes on the Christmas tree. Today the principal town making Christmas-tree decorations is Lauscha, where the glass-industry museum has many examples to show. Emigrants carried the delicate techniques round the world. At the same time improvements in paper folding and cutting made possible the intricate festoons, paper chains, bells, balls, birds and angels still sold by the million every Christmas for home and tree.

A finely worked straw goat, in the manner of a corn dolly, is found among Swedish decorations. A friend explained to one recipient that it would, as the god Thor's favoured beast, guard the Christmas tree and presents on Christmas Eve. Thor, a cheerful red-bearded god, had a chariot pulled by two he-goats. Should Thor fall short of food when travelling, he would kill, cook and eat the goats. Then next morning, when he waved his hammer (*Mjolnir*) over their hides, they sprang up good as new.

The emphasis on light at Christmas, associated by Christians with the Light of the World, is a solstitial survival. In Germany the wrought-iron *Schwibbogen* or 'Arch of Light', with red candles burning, stands over the gateway to the home. Lights have reached their apogee in the United States, where 20 foot (6.1 metre) lighted set pieces of Santa Claus with sleigh and reindeer bound over houses, town halls, shopping centres, even churches, lawns and rooflines, for weeks before Christmas. Rather sadly, United States Air Force personnel, stationed with Royal Air Force Strike Command at High Wycombe, Buckinghamshire, about 1960 lighted up their favourite decorations which they had brought with them. They quickly found that they had fallen foul of Britain's strict town-planning laws. They were not displaying a seasonal decoration but 'an unauthorised illuminated sign'.

Decorated trees in public places are a commonplace. They are increasingly being joined by decorated trees in private gardens and lawns, offering a seasonal greeting to passers-by. Thompson & Morgan's seed catalogue for 1992 recommended that gardeners grow their own Christmas tree and decorate it with coloured lights out of doors — 'an increasingly popular trend'.

6
CHRISTMAS CARDS

Refreshingly, for few things about Christmas are so clear-cut, the history of Christmas cards is both short and easily traced. Cards, so familiar today, date only from the mid nineteenth century. German influence has been strong but Christmas cards seem to be essentially an English invention.

The church had suppressed the Roman New Year *strenae* or gifts, along with other pagan practices. Seasonal gifts re-emerged only in the fifteenth century with German greetings cards called *Andachtsbilder* — devotional pictures for the home, decorated with a scroll, the Holy Child bearing a cross and the words *Ein gut selig Jar* ('A good and blessed year').

A New Year greeting; a woodcut of about 1467. Such woodcuts were among the ancestors of the modern Christmas card.

The first Christmas card, designed by J. C. Horsley RA for Sir Henry Cole in 1843.

For two centuries such cards grew rarer, until the late eighteenth century. Then they began to reappear, but now without religious significance and as a seasonal visiting card for friends. If the friends were away from home it was simple to scribble a greeting on the card and to leave it. Austria, Germany and France made lavish use of the cards; Vienna, in particular, became a production centre for them in the late eighteenth century and was followed by Berlin. Silk cards, or, for the less affluent, paper-lace fringes, were the taste of the age. The Berlin Iron Foundry even sent its customers cards made of cast iron.

Another ancestor was the eighteenth-century 'Christmas Piece', laboriously written on coloured paper at school by small children to show their parents how well they were progressing and to present their seasonal compliments. The pieces were carried home to become part of the family decorations.

The real instigator of Christmas cards seems to have been Sir Henry Cole (1808-82), writer and Chairman of the Society of Arts, who suggested a Christmas card to the artist John Calcott Horsley (1817-1903). In 1846 only a thousand cards were printed but the pattern for the future was formed. Over the following fifty years Christmas cards were to sweep the world, helped in England by the introduction by Sir Rowland Hill of the penny post and by the halfpenny post in 1870. A few years later Christmas cards reached the United States.

Progress in printing techniques continued, particularly in Germany, whose novelties included perspective views of snowy Alpine villages. By the 1860s familiar subjects were appearing: Christmas feasts, church bells, snowbound mail-coaches, children feeding birds, turkeys and plum puddings, lanterns, robins in the snow, the Christmas tree, the waits calling — nostalgia for Dickensian good cheer craved by many and enjoyed by few. The disturbing world of the twentieth century has merely confirmed the longing for such scenes.

In countries once strongly influenced by Britain, such as Australia and New Zealand, British card motifs survive, although robins are never seen and snow seldom. The United States has a parallel tradition with such favourite prints as the scenes of nineteenth-century American life by Currier and Ives. White New England churches, with their lights streaming across the snow and cutters (light, horse-drawn sleighs) waiting at the door, and pictures of poinsettias with dark green leaves and scarlet bracts are always popular.

The seasonal goodwill inherent in sending Christmas cards has been carried over into buying them: a large proportion of the Christmas cards bought in Britain are sold by or on behalf of charities such as Oxfam and the Save the Children Fund as well as many smaller ones. There are also charity seals for cards and letters. Denmark is particularly famous for her seals. Well over fifty million are sold each year. One year a very successful set of musical angels was designed by Queen Margrethe of Denmark, a talented artist.

St Nicholas arrives by boat in Amsterdam on 6th December, St Nicholas's Day. His servants, all called Black Peter, are with him. (Netherlands Board of Tourism.)

7
THE GIFTBRINGERS

Christmas gifts arrive with a mysterious Giftbringer who has travelled from afar. He may be St Nicholas, the Christchild, Santa Claus, Father Christmas, the Three Kings, the strange Knecht Rupprecht or the menacing Befana of Italy. There are others, some escorted by a train of demons or animals. The Giftbringer (owing much to Odin) arrives from the far north, a far country or perhaps Heaven, after a journey on horseback or in a reindeer sleigh, dog or goat carriage, often by night. Entry down the chimney puts him squarely on the magical hearth, heart of the house. There he will find the children's stockings or shoes, waiting to be filled with gifts.

Like the gods who were his forebears, the Giftbringer examines hearts and reads thoughts, approving the good and, in principle at least, disciplining the naughty. This sinister side of his character is now nearly forgotten in England and America. There is little but mindless beaming benevolence in the American Santa Claus or the British Father Christmas, but in Europe his judgemental qualities are still remembered.

St Nicholas of Patara, Bishop of Myra

St Nicholas, Bishop of Myra in the fourth century, Christendom's most popular saint, is patron of sailors, merchants, parish clerks, scholars, pawnbrokers and little boys, since he brought back to life three about to be pickled as bacon.

In west and south Germany, Switzerland, Holland, Belgium and Austria 6th December, St Nicholas's Day, is children's day and of far greater significance than Christmas Day. It is the day for presents but sometimes the saint preaches briefly and hears catechisms before he begins the distribution. In a custom with many variations, found in the Alpine regions of Europe, Bishop Nicholas, clad in episcopal robes and mitre and accompanied by his servant Black Peter, the Christmas Angel and *Perchten* mummers in hideous masks and garb, makes his round during the Christmas season. The mummers, named from Perchta or Berchta (spellings vary), goddess of the pagan Germans, march through the villages scaring badly behaved children and rewarding the good with nuts, apples and sweets from Peter's basket. There are mysterious aspects. Who, for example, are the two enigmatic straw-swathed 'ghosts of the field', cracking heavy whips to clear the saint's way? Other escorts include one who chastises wrong-doers with a birch rod and yet another creature in a horned goat's mask who bleats at the doors of those women deemed to have erred. A joke today, in earlier centuries this must have been a moment full of fear and menace. But St Nicholas's benign and dignified red and gold church presence and that of his servant Black Peter defeat the demons.

The party may be made up in many ways. The shaggy-horned Klaubauf with fiery eyes and long red tongue has clanking chains; in Lower Austria the rod carrier is the Krampus; in Styria the Bartel. Female bogeys appear: in Swabia the Berchtel; in Lower Austria the Budelfrau; near Augsburg the Buzebergt, starch pot and brush ready to smear faces. Their pedigree is muddled but decidedly heathen. But holy reinforcements are ready: Christ himself, St Peter, the Angel Gabriel, the Christchild and St Nicholas are at hand to help.

In another Alpine custom on 6th December at Küssnacht, Lake Lucerne, Switzerland, a procession of local revellers in lighted head-dresses races through the village, engaged on a 'hunt for St Nicholas' with whip cracking, clanging cowbells and trumpet blasts to help them.

On Christmas Night, sometimes alone, saying that Christ has sent him, and sometimes accompanying St Nicholas, appears the mysterious Knecht Rupprecht, whose origins are obscure. He is roughly dressed in skins and straw and, if appearing as Ru-Klas or 'Rough Nicholas', or Bullerklas, carries bells and chains and the statutory bag of Yule-log ashes, a useful accessory for one so close to the hearth. Or the task falls to St Nicholas disguised as Aschenklaus, with *his* Yule ashes. Another member of the party may be the white horse or Schimmel, with his rider. Sometimes he is intended to represent Woden. Equally elusive is the Pennsylvanian Germans' Pelznickel or 'Fur Nicholas', who, despite his name, is not St Nicholas but really his servant. He wears old fur-trimmed clothes, has a white beard, carries toys and rod and performs the usual praise and punishment role. 'Look out! He'll get you,' is the Christmas warning to the misbehaving.

On 6th December the shops of Holland and Belgium are full of marzipan fruits and animals, gingerbread and toys. Some parents still dress up as St Nicholas to ask penetrating questions about misdemeanours. Before the saint's visit the children set shoes and clogs full of hay for the saint's good white horse (a steed shared with Odin) and, in the Tirol, schnaps for Black Peter. In the morning the fodder has gone and sweets fill the shoes. As a plain hint, a bad child finds a rod by his shoes — and the hay is untouched. In Switzerland and parts of Germany and Austria St Nicholas speaks of packing miscreants in his sack and carrying them back to Spain. Somehow this never happens and all are given sweets!

In Amsterdam, with its great maritime tradition, St Nicholas arrives by boat before mounting his horse to make his rounds. The saint is accompanied by his Moorish servants in sixteenth-century Spanish dress and all are called Black Peter or Zwarte Piet. They throw gingerbread to an appreciative crowd. Church bells ring, bands play, civic dignitaries forgather and St Nicholas has a police escort.

Dutch Christmas presents have a special touch. A *Sinterklaas* poem, which must rhyme, hint at the gift and provide some illuminating comments on the recipient's character, is required. Under the Saint's benevolent protection some plain speaking is permitted!

The Christchild

In Catholic countries the Christchild or *Christkind* came to the fore at the Reformation and has always eclipsed Santa Claus in importance. He or she is a messenger on behalf of the soon-to-be-born Divine Child, but also a mythical figure little resembling the Holy Child of religious art. He is tall, a child, not a baby, often played by a girl with long fair hair, in white, a blend of child and angel, the good fairy and star which glitter on the Protestant Christmas tree.

In Alsace the Christchild, in a gold paper crown with candles, holds a silver bell and a basket of sweets. Her escort is the alarming Hans Trapp, with black face, bearskin, long beard and birch rod. In the familiar way he seeks out the badly behaved but the Christchild saves them. In Switzerland the Christkindli, a radiant angel, drives through the mountains in a six-deer sleigh. As the child enters the house, the Christmas tree is lighted, she distributes presents and her companions sing carols until it is time to move on. Nuremberg children receive some of their presents from the Christchild at the *Christkindlesmarkt*.

Guided by the light streaming out, the Christchild enters the German home through a window left open for her. The children wait in the next room, then the door opens and they are admitted. The cold draught from the open window and the blowing curtains make it easy to 'see' a shimmering departing figure. The ritual of dressing up as the Christchild is fading but children are still shown the open window and invited to test the draught; imagination does the rest. In France it is *le petit Jésus* who brings gifts.

The Christchild distributes gifts in a few ethnic communities in the United States, such as Zoar, Ohio, but the only real trace is Kriss Kringle (*Christkindl* in the American tongue), who in Pennsylvania's German communities has a role as a minor Giftbringer.

A Christmas masque at the court of Charles II. Father Christmas and the mummers carry the wassail bowl.

Santa Claus or Father Christmas

The appearance of Santa Claus or Father Christmas, whose day is 25th December, owes much to Odin, the old blue-hooded, cloaked, white-bearded Giftbringer of the north, who rode the midwinter sky on his eight-footed steed Sleipnir, visiting his people with gifts. Minor solstitial deities went with him. Gradually the lesser gods were lost, but Odin, transformed into Father Christmas, then Santa Claus, prospered and with St Nicholas and the Christchild became a leading player on the Christmas stage.

In the fifteenth century house doors had opened at Christmas to a cry of 'Welcome Old Father Christmas!'; then he appeared alike in mumming plays and court masques. Driven underground in England by the Puritans from 1644, he emerged triumphantly at the Restoration of 1660 as the revived 'Spirit of Christmas Rejoicing', a role he was to play brilliantly for the next three hundred years. In the nineteenth century, under Prince Albert's tutelage, he took on Teutonic character, acquiring new skills as night rider, sleigh driver, chimney descender, stocking filler, Giftbringer *par excellence*, resident of department stores and darling of the advertising industry.

It was in the United States that modern Santa Claus evolved, blending Old Father Christmas from England, the St Nicholas of Hessian troops and Dutch immigrants — and more than a hint of the rotund, smiling elf of northern Europe. The new image was developed by verses called 'The Visit of St Nicholas' written for his children on 23rd December 1822 by Clement Clark Moore, a professor of divinity. The public loved it and it has never faltered. To this day the rollicking words have a compulsive rhythm. They have passed into legend and annual recitation is imperative to any proper appreciation of the Christmas season:

'Twas the night before Christmas, when all through
    the house
Not a creature was stirring, not even a mouse;
The stockings were hung by the chimney with care,
In hopes that St Nicholas soon would be there;
The children were nestled all snug in their beds,
While visions of sugar-plums danced through their
    heads;
And mamma in her kerchief, and I in my cap,
Had just settled our brains for a long winter's nap, —
When out on the lawn there arose such a clatter,
I sprang from my bed to see what was the matter.
Away to the window I flew like a flash,
Tore open the shutters and threw up the sash.
The moon, on the breast of the new-fallen snow,
Gave a lustre of midday to objects below;
When what to my wondering eyes should appear,
But a miniature sleigh and eight tiny reindeer,
With a little old driver, so lively and quick
I knew in a moment it must be St Nick.
More rapid than eagles his coursers they came,
And he whistled and shouted and called them by
    name:
'Now, Dasher! now, Dancer! now, Prancer and Vixen!
On, Comet! on, Cupid! on, Donner and Blitzen!
To the top of the porch, to the top of the wall!
Now, dash away, dash away, dash away all!'
As dry leaves that before the wild hurricane fly,
When they meet with an obstacle, mount to the sky,
So, up to the house-top the coursers they flew,
With a sleigh full of toys, — and St Nicholas too.
And then in a twinkling I heard on the roof
The prancing and pawing of each little hoof,
As I drew in my head and was turning around,
Down the chimney St Nicholas came with a bound.
He was dressed all in fur from his head to his foot,
And his clothes were all tarnished with ashes and
    soot;

A bundle of toys he had flung on his back,
And he looked like a pedlar just opening his pack.
His eyes how they twinkled! his dimples how merry!
His cheeks were like roses, his nose like a cherry;
His droll little mouth was drawn up like a bow,
And the beard on his chin was as white as the snow.
The stump of a pipe he held tight in his teeth,
And the smoke it encircled his head like a wreath.
He had a broad face, and a little round belly
That shook, when he laughed, like a bowl full of jelly.
He was chubby and plump, — a right jolly old elf —
And I laughed when I saw him, in spite of myself.
A wink of his eye and a twist of his head
Soon gave me to know I had nothing to dread.
He spoke not a word, but went straight to his work,
And filled all the stockings; then turned with a jerk,
And laying his finger aside of his nose,
And giving a nod, up the chimney he rose.
He sprang to his sleigh, to his team gave a whistle,
And away they all flew like the down of a thistle;
But I heard him exclaim, ere he drove out of sight;
'Happy Christmas to all, and to all a good-night!'

The next milestone in image-making was Thomas Nast's drawing in 1863 in *Harper's Illustrated Weekly* of Dr Moore's creation,
clad not in the hooded robe of old Father Christmas, but in red
close-fitting combinations with wide leather belt and round fur hat
with a holly or mistletoe sprig (later to become a tasselled cap).
The figure, which Nast named Santa Claus, was not tall, dignified
and saint-like, but small, paunchy and gnomish, with white whiskers and sleigh. The European Giftbringer had arrived variously, by
horse, dog team, goat cart or camel. Nast introduced reindeer. His
father was Bavarian and his plump, elf-like Santa Claus, with
crimped beard and Germanic pipe, which he smoked while he
waited on the rooftop for the children to go to sleep, recalls this
inspiration. It appears on the cover of this book.

By now Santa Claus had two costumes: the old English red-
hooded robe, trimmed with white fur, and the distinctive American
belted combinations of Nast's imagination, more suggestive of a
Scandinavian *Tomte*. With a few variations (such as a hip-length
fur-trimmed jacket and trousers for wearing comfort) these distinc-
tions generally continue, although less marked than they were a
hundred years ago. Advertisers seem to favour American dress. In
England Father Christmas remains traditional. London theatrical
costumiers are reported to have for hire some fifty Father Christ-

mas outfits with hooded suits for every twenty American Santa Claus sets. (In the United States this would obviously be reversed.) But despite this allegiance to tradition little in Santa Claus's dress remains static; in Hawaii he arrives in a dugout canoe — wearing a red and white lava-lava (grass skirt)!

Another cornerstone of American tradition is the 'Virginia letter', which appeared in the *New York Sun*. A small girl of eight questioned the editor: 'Please tell me the truth; is there a Santa Claus?' She received a firm reply: 'Nobody sees Santa Claus but that is no sign that there is no Santa Claus,' — surely a sublime utilisation of the premise 'absence of evidence is not evidence of absence'?

It is civil to reward Giftbringers. Stella Johnson wrote to the *Halifax Chronicle-Herald* in 1975 of 'Santa's lunch' of home-made fruit cake and fat raisin buns which she and her sisters as children in Newfoundland prepared for Santa Claus. They were told that Santa called at the 'outports' (remote coastal fishing villages) on his way from the North Pole and would be looking forward to his meal. Mrs Johnson recalled the children's excitement next morning in touching the very crockery that Santa Claus had used in the night.

Santa Claus arrives at Bondi Beach, New South Wales. (Australian Tourist Commission.)

Santa Claus at home with reindeer at Rovaniemi, Finnish Lapland. The Finnish Giftbringer was red-clad Joulupukki or 'Christmas Spirit'. Today he often blends with Santa Claus. (Olavi Keskinen, Rovaniemi.)

Santa Claus at home

Santa Claus has several homes to which he retires to rest between seasons, to indulge his hobby of toymaking and to reply to his extensive correspondence. Among others the Swedes and Icelanders lay claim to him; Greenlanders have declared Uummannaq as his official residence and an extension to the Santa Claus Centre is planned. There he receives thirty thousand letters a year from children. Each receives a reply in English, Danish and Eskimo, with a message and small gift. The mountain Korvatunturi in Finnish Lapland is another Santa Claus home. He receives there 600,000 letters each year. They are answered by postal elves and should be addressed to: Arctic Circle, SF 96930, Rovaniemi, Finland.

The Arctic Circle is some 5 miles (8 km) north of the town of Rovaniemi, where Santa Claus presides in a log cabin with grazing reindeer in a snowy landscape at the door. Rovaniemi was rebuilt after the Second World War to Alvar Aalto's design, in which the roads follow the shape of reindeer antlers.

Despite the lack of a visible Santa Claus home in Britain the Post Office in 1991 received 750,000 letters addressed to him, including five in Braille from blind children. Braille replies were sent. The Canadian Post Office also receives thousands of letters for Santa Claus and millions of letters addressed to the Upper Austrian village of Christkindl have been forwarded by the Austrian Post Office.

The town of Santa Claus in the hills of south Indiana has suitably named roads such as Kriss Kringle Street, Christmas Tree Lane and Three Kings; and lakes named Christmas, Noël and Holly. A 42 ton giant painted statue of Santa Claus and many illuminated signs tell the story. There is even a golfing Santa Claus, it is said.

The commercial Santa Claus

The Santa Claus of commerce is found today in every department store and shopping mall. A California agency runs tough training sessions for would-be Santas. Students memorise the reindeers' names (as given in Moore's poem), learn how to say 'Ho, ho, ho!' without terrifying their infant clients and remember to use mouthwash. There are essential points to learn: whiskers, for example, should be fixed in place with carpet glue lest an inquisitive child give an experimental tug.

Berlin's Free University has run a students' 'Hire a Santa' service since 1949. Some five thousand Santas were booked in 1991 by parents to deliver children's presents in person with a song or a poem before vanishing with a well-chosen word about good behaviour. Girls can become Christmas Angels and Elves. Middle Eastern and North African students find themselves in great de-

Father Christmas entertains youthful admirers at Jenners of Edinburgh department store in Princes Street. (Jenners.)

mand. Children like their dark faces and the implication that they are world travellers by sleigh. The service is busiest on Christmas Eve afternoon, the traditional time for present-giving in Germany.

Other Giftbringers

Attention focuses on St Nicholas, the Christchild and Santa Claus as Giftbringers but there are many others. In Spain and western Provence, where there is no Santa Claus, the Magi ride to Bethlehem at Epiphany, passing every house in Spain on their way and leaving gifts. Children set their shoes on the windowsill with hay and barley for the horses or camels. The Kings respond. In Provence children set out to seek the Magi with hay for the horses and figs for the pages.

Today the Julebukk or 'Christmas Buck' of Norway and Denmark innocently echoes a pagan death-revival rite and the ancient belief that Thor brought presents in his goat wagon. By the middle ages the church objected to the pagan frolic of men in hides. It was suppressed but hung on as a harmless children's game in which goat-masked boys are rewarded as in the American 'trick and treat'.

Finland has no Santa Claus as such but the Joulupukki or 'Christmas Spirit', as Giftbringer, appears as a white-bearded, red-robed

68

figure, today indistinguishable from Santa Claus.

In Iceland during the twentieth century the Giftbringer's role was taken by the Jólasveinar or 'Christmas spirits', who came down from the mountains before Christmas, brought gifts and returned. Their activities included fomenting domestic ructions and eating naughty children. Personal characteristics varied; there was the Stiff-Necked Sheep-Chaser; Gorge Oaf, who stole milk from idle dairymaids; Shorty, who stole kitchen pans and licked them clean; the Sausage-Stealers, fond of Christmas smoked meats; the Pot-Licker or Pot-Scraper; Sniffer, who could find food at a distance and who even stole from the pets' bowls; Candle-beggar, who stole candles left burning at night; and Meat-Hooker, who reached down chimneys to steal racks of smoking meat.

Among the night trolls who menaced Icelandic children, good or naughty, were Grýla, her husband and large family, who controlled the Christmas festivities and who lived conveniently near to the family birch rod. Their power to scare has faded but wicked children may still be warned: 'If you land in Grýla's bag at Advent, you will be — literally — in the soup at Christmas!'

The gnome-like Swedish Jultomte lives under the barn and guards the livestock and farm. To preserve *Tomten* goodwill the wise householder leaves them a plate of porridge and milk (which they relish) at night, with perhaps clothes, spirits and tobacco. The *Tomte* enters after dinner on Christmas Eve to distribute presents from the tree.

Tomten are classic Christmas-card subjects. Typically in one design a white-whiskered *Tomte* in pointed red hat drives a four-dog sledge of presents past a snowbound farm, where the Christmas sheaf waits on its post for the birds. In another a smiling *Tomte* watches a small girl and boy as they set his bowl of porridge in the stable. The Swedish artist Jenny Nyström has made hundreds of Christmas cards of *Tomten* subjects and may even be said to have created their image, as Nast created the image of Santa Claus.

In Norway the Giftbringer is the Julenisse, an elf-like figure with white beard and red cap. *Rommegröt* (porridge) must be left in the attic or on the doorstep on Christmas Eve to win his favour for the year. Usually he eats until his buttons fly, then he falls asleep, often in an old shoe or somebody's hat. The *rommegröt* meal has been linked with the 4000-year-old belief that the dead return to their former homes at Yule. The living fed them but took care to remain indoors themselves.

The mysterious *Frau*, under various names, whose preoccupation with spinning makes her obsolete today, rules German lore. Frau Holda or Holle in central Germany and Austria, Frau Berchta or Perchta in southern Germany and the Tirol, Frau Frick or Freen in the north down to the Harz Mountains, Frau Gaude or Gode, Frau Harke and other names, is dreaded rather than loved, generous in rewarding those who serve her and in punishing the lazy. Girls must finish spinning by Christmas. If Frau Berchta finds flax on a distaff she is angered. In Carinthia they mark *Berchteltag* at Epiphany, when a strange skin-clad Berchtel prances in the streets.

In Mecklenburg on the Twelve Nights Gode enjoys driving her dog train through villages. If she sees a front door standing open she sends a little dog through it; he wags his tail, settles in and will not be driven away, turning into a stone by day and a dog by night. All the year he whines and brings ill-luck to the house. Careful people keep doors tightly shut during the Nights. However, Gode generously rewards those who have served her. A peasant repaired her carriage pole and found as he worked that the wood chips falling from his adze turned to pure gold.

Holde is the most friendly of the *Frauen*, driving in Saxony on New Year's Eve with a carriage full of gifts to villages that had shown her respect. In Hesse and Thuringia she is imagined as a beautiful woman in white with long golden hair. Snow was described as 'Frau Holde shaking her feather bed'.

In Sicily *la Vecchia di Natali*, the 'Christmas Old Woman', brings gifts on Christmas Eve. Or they may arrive at New Year at the hands of old St Strina (descended from the goddess Strenia) or in the north from St Lucia. Sometimes the children's presents come at Epiphany from Befana, who acquires her name from Epiphania. She is female, benign yet malevolent, half witch, half good fairy, loved and feared but also almost revered and carried in processions. For the good she leaves presents in stockings, and for the bad stones or ashes. Italian toy shops and pastrycooks often encourage their staff to dress as Befana to amuse child customers. Legend related that she was told of the Magi's coming but was too busy with housework to greet them. Now she wanders disconsolately from house to house watching for the Kings with conciliatory presents. She enters down the chimney, a sure sign of her antiquity.

In the *Julklapp*, a distinctive Swedish and north German way of giving presents, the gift is wrapped in many layers of paper. Disguise is all-important. A tiny gold ring may rest in a huge box. Without warning and with only a teasing rhyme as an accompaniment, the gift is tossed through the door at speed. Famous stories tell of girls who receive bulky *Julklapps* which turned out to be ardent, well-wrapped lovers. A classic story tells of Major Jones of Georgia who spent the night on his sweetheart's porch so well wrapped and tied that he was barely able to fend off the investigations of the family dog, which spent the whole night attacking him.

8
CHRISTMAS GAMES AND AMUSEMENTS

While the Yule log crackled on the British hearth the company dived for apples in tubs of water, jumped to the ceiling for treacle buns and played games such as 'hot cockles' and 'hunt the slipper', 'musical chairs' and 'blind man's buff'. In the early eighteenth century the author of *Round Our Coal-Fire, or Christmas Entertainments* wrote: 'Dancing is one of the chief exercises, or else there is a match of Questions and Commands ... most of the other diversions are cards and dice.'

In 'snapdragon', played on Christmas Eve, with the room in darkness, brandy was poured over raisins in a large shallow dish and lighted. The players tried to snatch flaming raisins despite their burned fingers. In the west of England the more modest 'flapdragon' was played, when a lighted candle was placed in a cider can and the contents were drunk by the players, if possible without setting themselves on fire — a feat in the days of Victorian side whiskers.

The Lord of Misrule (in France, *Abbé de la Malgouverné*; in Scotland, the Abbot of Unreason), essential to celebrations of Christmas in the middle ages, was a master of ceremonies elected

Snapdragon, a game that was part of every Victorian Christmas. In this scene of 1858 the boys are the most daring players while Uncle George licks his burnt fingers. Drawn by C. Keene.

to preside until Twelfth Night over the games and forfeits and other Christmas revels, particularly those of the royal court, the Inns of Court or the great houses. It resembled the role of the master of the Roman *Saturnalia*. Church leaders regarded the Lord as an encouragement to licence and grossness. He was particularly resented by the Puritans and did not survive the seventeenth century in his original form.

Crackers

Christmas crackers would delight any Lord of Misrule, with hats and crowns for the masquerade, flashes and bangs to frighten evil spirits, even a touch of motto clairvoyance. Indispensable to the Christmas table, the cracker, a decorated paper tube, wrapped in coloured papers and tinsel, with a friction strip to 'pop' when the cracker breaks between the two persons who pull it, was invented by Tom Smith in 1847. Today his company, based in Norwich, produces 50 million crackers each year and exports to some fifty countries.

The magic lantern was another Victorian parlour favourite. This optical instrument passed a light through a picture painted on a glass plate and projected an image on to a convenient wall. (Drawn by H. G. Hine.)

The Lord of Misrule and his page acted as masters of ceremonies for the twelve days of Christmas.

Tom Smith devised the cracker by his own log fire, basing it on the form of a wrapped sweet and adding a friction strip and a small present. Paper hats, topical mottoes and specialist boxes reflecting current events, such as the Paris Exhibition (1900), Votes for Women, the Channel Tunnel (the original version) and Charlie Chaplin, came later.

Mumming

Mumming, the performance in costume of an ancient folk play in the street or in the inn, was, and to a small extent still is, an inseparable part of the old English Christmas. It was not an amusement as such but a ritual well over one thousand years old, linked with pagan rites celebrating the triumph of light over darkness together with sacrifices to the harvest spirit. The players, with blackened faces hidden by streamers, wore costumes of paper. Stock characters, some in place since the Crusades, are St George, the Turkish Knight and the Doctor. St George and the Knight fight

A party of mummers. (From Chambers 'Book of Days', 1864.)

Mummers at the door. St George, riding the hobby-horse, has the dragon at his feet.

The mummers, seen here at Marshfield, Avon, wear traditional costumes of paper strips and ribbons. Once their faces were kept hidden. The Marshfield play is still performed each year. (Brian Shuel.)

and the one killed is revived by the Doctor, who wears a top hat and striped trousers. In Lincolnshire the characters Wild Work, Elsie Belsie Bug (or Beelzebub) and Allspice showed themselves and in other plays Little Devil Doubt, Happy Jack, Oliver Cromwell and even Nelson and Napoleon appear.

As a natural consequence of a long line of kings St George became King George in some plays and in Philadelphia it is George Washington who slays the dragon:

> Here I am Great Washington
> On my shoulders I carry a gun...

from the English model:

> In comes I, Beelzebub
> Over my shoulder I carries my club...

Father Christmas appears:

> In comes I, Old Father Christmas,
> Welcome or welcome not,
> I hope Old Father Christmas,
> Will never be forgot...

Although the players were village boys, known to all present, a shadow of the former mystery and magic clung to them as they clattered in, disguised, from the frosty lanes. Even in the nineteenth century it was felt unwise to name them; it still is in Newfoundland, where mumming survives, although as a house visit rather than as a play. The Newfoundland players wore pasteboard hats with the costliest wallpapers and richest ribbons hiding their faces in time-honoured anonymity.

'Devils', 'Death' and 'Bears' from the Guisers' Procession at Koniaków-Rupienka, Poland.

Usually in 'revived' form, the traditional mumming play could be seen in the following places at Christmas 1991: St Albans, Hertfordshire; Gloucester; Moulton, Northamptonshire; Marshfield (Waterley Bottom), Avon; and Crookham, Hampshire. Crookham has had a mumming play for one hundred years at least. The Marshfield play, too, is of some antiquity and was revived in 1924.

In northern Greece mumming is common between New Year's Day and Epiphany, with characters such as the Bride and Groom, Granny and the Moorish Sea Captain. Beginning on St Nicholas's Eve, several groups of 'guisers' — 'bears', 'bulls' and 'ancestors' — perform at Koniaków-Rupienka in Poland, with characters of Nobleman and Serfs, Butcher, Devils, Chimney Sweep, Priest, Doctor, and Man in Goat's Mask. The players chase bystanders with forks; the grooms and horses prance. Householders give them wine and vodka with a Christmas offering for the priest. The guisers visit and bring luck only to those who welcome them. In Silesia they are called the 'Nicholas Procession'.

Half a world away and far more splendidly outfitted, yet clearly with similar roots to English custom, is the spectacle of the Philadelphia Mummers' Day Parade in Pennsylvania. This lasts a long New Year's Day from early to late. Thousands of spectators, often braving bitter weather, wait beside the street to admire the spectacular costumes, music, acting and polished clowning of the masked players. Huge sums may be spent on costumes; a robe may extend the whole width of Broad Street with perfectly matched attendants to carry it. The *Philadelphia Daily News* reported of the 55th parade in 1955 that 'four Fancy Clubs, five Comic Clubs and twenty-one String Bands', in costumes worth over $300,000 and taking six hours to pass a given point, would 'strut' in the parade, including 52 pages of the 'Olde English Court'. The following day the *Philadelphia Inquirer* reported twelve thousand marchers. Characters vary, reflecting current events and topics; but a few appear regularly and here the roots are English — 'The Prince of Egypt' 'St George and the Dragon' (St George appearing, naturally, as George Washington). A famous couplet,

In comes I, Little Devil Doubt,
And with my brush I'll sweep you all out,

is said to have crossed the Atlantic to become:

Here comes I, Old Cooney Cracker,
I swear to God my wife chews terbacker.

At *Kalends* men ran through Roman streets masked and in skins with animal horns on their heads — proceedings roundly condemned by the church as objectionably pagan. Nevertheless, traces of the hobby-horse are still to be found in England and Wales, Austria, France, Belgium, Switzerland, Scandinavia and eastern Europe, although sometimes at seasons other than Christmas.

At Kingscote, Gloucestershire, a man with his head thrust into a bull's mask (the 'Christmas Bull') was, with his keeper, invited into every house for luck. None refused him. The Hooden Horse made his cavorting rounds in east Kent, dancing at every door. His body was swathed in a white sheet and his jaws opened and shut with a realistic snap. He could be an alarming sight; in 1835 the Horse was banned from Broadstairs for, it was said, frightening a woman to death. Two or three of the old figures have been found in recent years and are used in revivals.

In South Wales the custom of *Mari Lwyd* ('Grey Mare') continues at Pencoed, Mid Glamorgan. A horse's skull decorated with ribbons and glinting bottle-glass eye is carried on a long pole by a man concealed by the mandatory white sheet. His party includes Leader, Merryman, Punch, Judy and the Sergeant. Again and again the jaws snap in the winter dusk and the figure chases and bites everyone it can, releasing victims only in return for forfeits.

Pantomime

A traditional Christmas entertainment which has triumphantly kept its appeal in modern Britain is pantomime. Some authorities have detected connections with Saturnalian extravagances. Today pantomime is a very British affair but it had its beginnings when a group of French actors, complete with performing dogs, came to England in 1717. By 1758 the famous Grimaldi family of clowns had appeared. Pantomime finally became a sophisticated review with a thread of a fairy story as a plot. *Cinderella* (a piece said to bring luck to the cast) uses part of the story by Charles Perrault, the seventeenth-century French writer whose other fairy tales include *The Sleeping Beauty* and *Red Riding Hood*. *Aladdin* recalls the interest in the Far East in the tea-clipper age. Widow Twankey takes her name from the name of a tea the clippers were rushing home. Pantomimes have their own reputations: *Robin Hood* and *Babes in the Wood* are both unlucky and accidents are expected during the run. Pantomimes have become vehicles for gorgeous costumes, catchy songs, clowning, transformation scenes and the stage manager's every trick. A modern fancy is for leading roles to be played by personalities well known in other spheres as diverse as news reading and boxing.

London children know that the play *Peter Pan* is essential to Christmas. Written by Sir J. M. Barrie (1860-1937), the novelist and dramatist, it was first produced at the Duke of York's Theatre in 1904, with the now world-famous characters of Nana, the dog-nurse, Peter Pan, Wendy, Tinkerbell, the flying fairies, Captain

Hook, the pirates Smee and Starkey, and the crocodile with the eight-day clock inside him. Some thought Barrie mad to hope for success with it but they were wrong; the play has been produced every Christmas since 1904, with each succeeding generation as an audience.

A nineteenth-century pantomime playbill.

The Memorial Church at Oberndorf, Austria, on the site of the church where the carol 'Silent Night', composed by Franz Gruber, with words by Father Mohr, was first performed in 1818. (Austrian National Tourist Office/Markowitsch.)

9
CHRISTMAS CAROLS

The word 'carol', from the Old French *carole*, a dance with a song, has had religious associations only since the fourteenth century. Earlier carols were sung at any feasting or celebration. The great age for English carol composition was from 1400 to 1650, when the Puritans characteristically suppressed them. For two hundred years carols were to be the songs of the unsophisticated. In 1826 William Hone wrote: 'they are ditties which now exclusivly enliven the industrious servant and the humble labourer.' This saved them. Later in the nineteenth century the Victorians, yearning for the Christmas of an earlier England, found them still remembered in the countryside and Cecil Sharp, the great collector of English folksong, rescued a number remaining only in the oral tradition.

The earliest printed collection of carols, by Wynkyn de Worde, appeared in 1521 and included the 'Boar's Head Carol', still sung today at Queen's College, Oxford, Indiana University's Madrigal Feast and the Empress Hotel, Victoria, British Columbia, and elsewhere. A number of popular carols contained clear hints of paganism: 'The Holly and the Ivy', expressing the male-female symbolism of the trees, was typical.

Most well-known carols sung today have been written since the eighteenth century. The words of 'While Shepherds Watched Their Flocks by Night' are by Nahum Tate (1632-1715). Charles Wesley wrote the first version of 'Hark the Herald Angels Sing' published in 1753. The words of 'Christians Awake! Salute the Happy Morn' are by John Byrom (1691-1763). 'O Little Town of Bethlehem', by the American Bishop Phillips Brooks (1835-93), was written for his Sunday school in 1868 and supposedly inspired by a ride from Jerusalem to Bethlehem. Gustav Holst's tune of 'In the Bleak Midwinter' (words by Christina Rossetti, 1830-94) was written in 1906. J. M. Neal's carol 'Good King Wenceslas' has made the saint's name familiar to everyone although the story in the carol is entirely imaginary. The earliest traceable date for the words and music of 'O Come All Ye Faithful' (*Adeste Fidelis*) is 1743. It was probably composed in France and came to English Roman Catholic churches in the eighteenth century. In 1797 it was sung at the Portuguese embassy and became known as 'The Portuguese Hymn'.

Perhaps the most famous of all carols, 'Silent Night', composed by Franz Gruber (1787-1863), the organist, to verses by Father Mohr, the village priest, of Oberndorf, Salzburg, Austria, was first

Victorian child carol singers: a favourite cartoon by 'Phiz'.

sung at the old St Nikolas's church in 1818. This was destroyed by a flood in 1899. A memorial chapel stands at the site and here, and in the new St Nikolas's church, the carol can be heard during Midnight Mass on Christmas Eve.

Cecil Sharp owed much to groups such as the town waits, who carried old carols in retentive memories. In the eighteenth century the waits, carrying their oboes, serpents, clarinets and fiddles, went from door to door, singing when all were in bed. They had begun as watchmen calling the hours of the night but at Christmas turned to music and 'walked the parish', playing outside citizens' houses and being rewarded. Because of their former role, they frequently sang during the night, at Cambridge at the difficult hour of two o'clock. Washington Irving was charmed by a group he met during his visit to Yorkshire in 1820. He heard music and, looking sleepily down into the dark garden, found 'it proceeding from a band, which I concluded to be the waits from some neighbouring village. They went round the house, playing under the windows. The sounds, as they receded, became more soft and aerial, and seemed to accord with quiet and moonlight.'

Today singers may still come to the door, but more frequently groups sing in a public place such as a shopping centre, a market place or round a communal Christmas tree. A correspondent in *The Times* wrote with sadness of the paucity of carol singers in the countryside today: 'Nights are silent, now we lack this Hardy perennial' (referring to the village musicians in Thomas Hardy's novels). But Andrew Sewell of Aldbourne, Wiltshire, was able to correct him on 2nd January 1992:

> The combined churches' choir toured the village on several nights … the village band, descended from the church musicians evicted when an organ was installed well over 150 years ago, called here and elsewhere on Christmas Eve with our favourite carol; it then serenaded the village, starting at 4 a.m. this morning with 'Christians Awake' and continuing until the church bells rang out at 7 a.m.

There were other visitors to the front door. The wassailers (*waes-heal* = 'good health!') came singing carols and carrying their legendary wassail bowl, of holly or maple wood with two arching iron bands over its top, decorated with ribbons and evergreens and filled at the doorstep by grateful householders. The bowl often held as much as 2 gallons (9 litres) of hot cider punch and the wassailers had their own song:

> Wassail! Wassail! All over the town,
> Our toast it is white, our ale it is brown
> Our bowl it is made of the maplin tree,
> We be good fellows, I drink to thee.

In a quieter wassailing custom a party of women and children

Just after 10 o'clock, on a wet night about 1853, the town waits, well muffled up, serenade the town. One carries a comforting bottle in his pocket. In the background a policeman listens, his bullseye lantern gleaming. (Engraved from a drawing by H. G. Hine.)

'The Wassail Bowl' from 'Punch', 29th December 1888.

carried round a so-called 'vessel-cup', a small box holding, on a bed of cut paper, muslin and ribbons, small figures of the Virgin and Holy Child. The box, covered with a sheet of glass and a white napkin, was shown on request. It was a clear echo of a Catholic, pre-Reformation practice and of the crib of European tradition. The favourite carol of the vessel-cup party was:

> Here we come a-wassailing
> Among the leaves so green
> Here we come a-carolling
> So fair to be seen
> God send you happy! God send you happy!
> God send you all a happy New Year.

The 'Holly Riders' of Exmoor rode on the stout native ponies of the district round the hill farms in Somerset with holly-wreathed hats and holding lanterns, singing for pennies, cakes and cider.

In Australia and New Zealand carollers sing by night in the public parks. In Alexandra Gardens, Melbourne, 400,000 singers may gather in summer weather. The first assembly was in 1937 but the real origins of the custom are thought to lie with the Cornish miners who gathered round Moonta in South Australia in the early days to sing Methodist hymns. Exiled Cornishmen followed the same custom in the mining town of Butte, Montana. Another 'carols by candlelight' concert takes place on the Arctic Circle at

Rovaniemi in Finnish Lappland.

The best-known of all carol services must be the Festival of the Nine Lessons and Carols in King's College Chapel, Cambridge, on Christmas Eve, familiar to thousands since it was first broadcast in 1930. Nine lessons are read, each by a different reader, and nine carols are sung, including the famous solo performance of 'Once in Royal David's City', which opens the service.

In the United States 'Christmas tree choirs' are popular. Choir members of the Eastside Baptist Church, Marietta, Georgia, dressed in Christmas angel-like cloaks with gleaming collars, arrange themselves as a 'living Christmas tree' inside the church, to sing carols. The 'tree' is beautifully dressed with gilded angels, bows, glass balls and other Christmas-tree decorations. At the top is a large glowing star.

In a long-established custom in Vancouver, Canada, carol music from 'carol boats', their rigging picked out with coloured lights reflected in the dark waters of the harbour, floats from the North to South Shores. Hundreds of carol singers with home-made paper lanterns climb 1 1/4 miles (2 km) up Squaw Peak, Phoenix, Arizona, to sing carols on the top, and another concert echoes underground

The Christmas Tree Choir of Eastside Baptist Church, Marietta, Georgia, USA. (Eastside Baptist Church.)

DITE AVE MARI

Calabrian shepherds (pifferari) pipe at a shrine to the Virgin Mary in Rome at Christmas. They were said to be piping away her labour pains.

through the longest known cave system in the world in Mammoth Cave National Park, Kentucky.

Greek boys singing the significantly named *Kalanda* carry round the message of Christmas goodwill. Their traditional accompaniment is a triangle and clay drum. They carry a spray of evergreen with which to tap the master of the house for luck and in return are given money, buns and nuts.

Rome and Naples once enjoyed a different form of music when the shepherds of Calabria, *pifferari*, came in from the country to play their pipes in front of shrines to the Virgin Mary. Usually two shepherds played the pipes and one the bagpipe or *zampogne*. They were said to be piping away the Virgin's labour pains.

10
THE CRIB

Focus of countless Christmas scenes in church, market, school and home, the nativity scene, *presepio*, *Krippe*, *crèche*, 'Bethlehem', *putz* or crib displays the familiar figure of the Holy Child laid in a stable manger surrounded by Mary, Joseph, the ox, the ass, shepherds and sheep and the Magi or Three Kings, grouped in worship. It is a sight particularly beloved by children. Since the scene is often arranged beneath the Christmas tree, Christian and pagan beliefs mingle.

The first crib is said to have been set up by St Francis of Assisi in Greccio in 1224, with a living ox and ass. On this first occasion Mary, Joseph and the shepherds were played by actors, although a wax model represented the Divine Infant. Today the most beautiful crib in Italy is said to be in the Franciscan church of Ara Coeli, Rome, where on a high platform in front of the *presepio* (Christmas landscape) children still stand to recite poems or to tell the story of *Gesu Bambino*, to the applause of admiring family and friends. The Bambino, whose flesh tint is said to be God-given,

The living crib from Outre-Meuse, Paroisse Saint-Pholien, 1936. (Musée de la Vie Wallonne, Liège.)

'Adoration of the Shepherds': early eighteenth-century to early nineteenth-century Neapolitan or presepio crib figures in wood and terracotta. The view is over the Gulf of Naples, with Vesuvius in the background.

crowned, swathed in gold and silver tissue and jewel-encrusted, is supposed to have miraculous powers. At Epiphany it is carried out into the streets and the city of Rome is blessed. Crib figures are an important purchase in Italian families. Sold in great numbers at the Piazza Navona market, they became heirlooms to be lovingly placed in home-made landscape settings, including the sacred cave with moss and straw for the Holy Child, stream, shepherds' hut and star. Singing angels are suspended on invisible wires. Seeding grasses and woodruff are used in the manger because, it is said, they formed the bedding of Mary and the Holy Child. In France the name for woodruff is *Fleur de la Ste-Vierge*.

At Les Baux, Provence, a centuries-old ritual, described by Alphonse Daudet, is performed. The midnight procession of the *fête des bergers* takes place on Christmas Eve in the twelfth-century church of St Vincent. In the past charges of paganism caused the authorities to try to suppress the ritual but it survives, to an accompaniment of Provençal music of flute and tambourine. The shepherds still offer their lambs to Christ at Midnight Mass.

The presepio was set up on a flat roof typical of Naples; the object was to make the painted and real landscapes seem as one. (Bayerisches Nationalmuseum, Munich.)

But despite undeniable piety, the custom's future is uncertain. In 1991 only four or five flocks of sheep remain in the area, where in 1980 there had been twenty. At Labastida, Spain, a similar ceremony takes place; a lamb and a baby representing Jesus are carried in. At midnight twelve shepherds enter the church, sing and dance and when mass is over make a bonfire and pretend to make soup for the Child. Living cribs are increasingly popular; a famous one in California, at the eighteenth-century Santa Barbara Mission Church, has live sheep and cows.

Indispensable to Christmas, particularly in Provence, are *santons* — 'little saints'. Every household had its crib and *santons* extend the range of characters far beyond the Holy Family. At the time of the French Revolution, when cribs were banned, the pious continued to set them up in the home. In Marseilles they took the form of miniature theatres with characters from village life: the butcher, baker, brigand, musician, knife-grinder and old women making *aioli* (the garlic-flavoured mayonnaise of Provence). Exhibitions of *santons* are held and families enlarge their collections at the market.

The finest crib-figure collection in the world is said to be at the Bavarian National Museum, Munich, with examples from Germany, Tirol and Italy. One made in Bozen in the early nineteenth century is large enough to fill a fair-sized room, representing the central square of a town with a large cathedral.

As befits a country whose people are notably skilled in wood-carving, Austria is well-known for the beauty of its cribs and figures. At Ebensee am Traunsee in the Salzkammergut the cribs, called *Ebenseer Landschaftskrippe*, have painted backgrounds showing the delectable scenery of woods, mountains and the Traunsee round the village. Some cribs show the manger set up within a ruinous castle or pagan temple, denoting the fresh start made when Christ was born and things pagan were swept away or diminished. Many Ebensee families make their own cribs, which are displayed from 25th December to 2nd February (Candlemas).

The crib in the Place de Marché forms the centrepiece of the *Village de Noël* in Liège, Belgium, and is blessed when the 'village' is opened in December. In 1991 the marionettist Claude Deletrez made a set of over a dozen crib figures for the village in

A crib from Ebensee am Traunsee, Austria. The background shows the distinctive landscape round the village. In traditional style the crib is set up in a ruined classical building symbolising a fresh start for man. In this scene the Magi arrive by elephant. (Ebensee am Traunsee Tourismusverband/Foto Reichl, Ebensee.)

*Szopka or crib made for the building trades annual crib-building com-
petition in Kraków, Poland, held just before Christmas. The cribs are
carried from house to house by children singing carols.*

91

the distinctive tradition of Liège marionettes. Each figure is over 3 feet 3 inches (1 metre) tall.

The crib usage has proved resilient. In Romania, after many years of communist rule, during which the celebration of Christmas was forbidden, in December 1991, the second anniversary of Nicolae Ceausescu's fall, a life-sized crib was set up in University Square, Bucharest. The Holy Child's frozen swaddling bands were laden with coins left there to solicit God's help in finding food.

Midnight Mass

Of the many Christmas services in churches the Midnight Mass on Christmas Eve is by far the most popular. The term is a Catholic one but it has been widely adopted by the Protestant churches for their own midnight services. Few services are more impressive, whether in the great cathedrals of Paris, Rome or Vienna or in a village church. In the Austrian Tirol the faithful, on foot and carrying blazing torches, make their way down the narrow valleys from houses and farms scattered in the pinewoods, moving slowly towards the village. The torches flickering between the trees and reflecting the snow, approach until the valley floor is reached. Then the torches are extinguished and only the windows of the church glow as the familiar opening words of the Christmas service are spoken.

In Sweden before dawn on Christmas morning the *Julotta* Mass is held, lighted by lanterns and candles. The congregation often comes to church by sleigh. Young men with flaming torches escorted their minister to the Welsh Protestant service of *Plygain* (Crowning of the Cock) at four o'clock on Christmas morning. The congregation had stayed in the church from the early hours until day-break, singing psalms and hymns to the light of coloured candles until the sun came up and Christmas Day really began.

For the Moravians in Bethlehem, Pennsylvania, where a huge eight-pointed star shines over the town, the service begins on Christmas Eve and ends at midnight. Candles burn in every corner and the congregation holds wax tapers in special holders. The custom began in 1741 when Count Nicholas von Zinzendorf, leader of the European Moravians, led his followers, holding candles, into a stable at Herrenhut to keep their Christmas vigil, as their descendants do today in a church.

11
THE FEAST OF STEPHEN

Meets of hounds and horse-racing link modern Boxing Day with the Feast of Stephen, 26th December. St Stephen, a Swedish missionary murdered by the heathen, became connected with horses, probably because he loved them and owned five which he would ride when he went out to preach. After his martyrdom one carried his body to burial and his grave became a place of pilgrimage for sick horses. In several northern European countries ceremonial rides took place and horses were bled and physicked on his day. An old rhyme told of:

> ... Saint Stephen's day, whereon doth every man
> His horses jaunt and course abrode as swiftly as he
> can,
> Until they doe extreemly sweate, and then they let
> them blood
> For this being done upon this day they say doth do
> them good
> And keepes them from all maladies and sicknesse
> through the yeare.

In the Tirol horses were fed consecrated salt, bread and oats and the priest blessed with holy water any animal brought to church. In Sweden at one o'clock in the morning horses were ridden to northward-flowing water to drink 'the cream of the river' and thus stay fit. Violent races took place to and from church. Then in the early morning groups of 'Stephen's Men' raced from village to village, waking the inhabitants with the song *Staffansvisa* — and expecting drinks in return. In Munich two hundred mounted men would ride decorated horses three times round the interior of a church, a custom surviving until 1876. The Finns threw a piece of silver into the horses' drinking trough to make them prosperous.

In England colourful Boxing Day meets are popular. Riders in hunting scarlet and top hats emphasise sociability rather than sport, with stirrup cups for riders and the village pub at hand for foot followers to drink healths. Horse-racing is equally important.

A variety of other sporting events from football to swimming and regattas also centre on Boxing Day. Members of Brighton Swimming Club take their traditional dip in the English Channel from Brighton Pier. At the Serpentine, Hyde Park, London, some thirty contestants compete in a 100 yard (91 metres) dash for the Peter Pan Cup, a trophy donated to the Serpentine Swimming Club in 1903 by the playwright Sir James Barrie (a club member), author of the favourite Christmas play *Peter Pan* (see pages 78-9). In 1870 the *Daily Telegraph* reported of the one- to four-minute swim: 'In no country but happy England could such a scene be witnessed as the breaking of 3 inches of ice to give enough water for the race to take place.' With air and water temperatures at one degree Celsius a woman swimmer led a procession of hardy souls through the icy waters of the Moldau in Prague at Christmas 1991.

A 'sporting' custom once widespread in England, and France and the Isle of Man, and perhaps still to be found in rural Ireland, was 'Hunting the Wren' on St Stephen's Day, 'Wrenning Day'.

Contestants for the Serpentine Swimming Club's Peter Pan Swimming Cup, presented by Sir J. M. Barrie, leave the water after the race on Boxing Day, watched by curious waterfowl. (A. W. Titmuss/Serpentine Swimming Club.)

'Hunting the Wren' in Ireland on St Stephen's Day about 1945.

The 'Wren Boys' hunted the bird, killed it and carried it round tied to the tip of a pole, asking for money from bystanders and handing out 'lucky' feathers if rewarded. These were a powerful charm against shipwreck.

In Victorian England 'Christmas boxes', presents, usually of money, were given on 26th December to those who had served the household in the year. Postmen, dustmen and errand boys were likely recipients. Boxing Day took its name from the custom, which was so called in the seventeenth century when the gifts were presented in earthenware boxes. These gifts were common in Britain until the Second World War but higher wages have made them largely obsolete. Perhaps a modern equivalent can be seen in the Christmas bonuses and hampers given by many firms to their employees.

12
THE NEW YEAR

Seeing in the New Year

The magic of fresh starts, of new hopes and resolutions for the future is powerful on the eve of the New Year. 'Seeing the New Year in' is a ritual enjoyed by crowds throughout the world, who watch the final minutes of the Old Year tick away in Trafalgar Square, London; Times Square, New York; Red Square, Moscow and Stefansplatz, Vienna. Clocks strike midnight, church bells peal, car horns, ships' sirens and factory hooters join in a great wave of sound.

While Germans wait for midnight to arrive they pass the time with *Feuerzangenbowle* ('firetongs punch') and the traditional accompaniment of apricot jam and cream doughnuts. *Sylvester-abend* (New Year's Eve) has a great air of anticipation. At midnight firecrackers rattle down the streets and drums beat. In Bavaria all house lights are turned off just before midnight; then, as the clock strikes, they are all switched on again in a great welcoming blaze of light. Knowledgeable travellers book flights across southern Germany just before midnight on *Sylvesterabend* to witness the drama of the lights.

On New Year's Day itself bakeries and *pâtisseries* sell *Neujahrs-kränze* ('New Year's wreaths') of various sizes. For afternoon coffee there are *Neujahrstorten*, often buttercream gâteaux decorated like a clock face or the page of a calendar.

In Holland the New Year provokes more cooking. Similar to the doughnuts called *Oliebollen* (deep-fried round buns sprinkled with sugar) are their variations, *Berlinerbollen*, filled with custard, and *Appelflappen*, containing fresh apples. These are all bought from street stalls and eaten on the spot.

A new custom may have been started in 1991. At midnight on 30th/31st December the top ten floors of Canary Wharf Tower in East London, at 800 feet (244 metres) Britain's tallest building, became a laser clock face recording the hours of 1991 still to run. At 11.59 pm the tower began the countdown to midnight and wished the New Year 'HI'. Fireworks exploded and 1992 began.

First footing

Public ceremonies over, in the north of England and Scotland the first-footers hurry away on their luck-carrying mission, to be the first person to enter (uninvited) their own homes or the homes of friends, as a New Year visitor. Often they carry lucky gifts of

Tar-barrel burning at Allendale, Northumberland, just before midnight on New Year's Eve. (Mark Hutchinson.)

bread, salt, coal, money and evergreens (emblematic of refreshment, wealth, warmth and longevity). It is a custom found in many forms across Europe. Rules (which vary with district) generally require that a first-footer be a man, a bachelor, dark-haired, not flat-footed or cross-eyed, not fair or red-haired (lest he be a pillaging Norseman, disguised). A generous 'hot pint' of mulled ale, whisky and nutmeg rewards his efforts.

The fire festivals

Evil spirits have always lurked about the joints of man's calendar, of which the New Year is clearly one. A number of Scottish and northern English towns and villages take care to burn out the Old Year and to welcome the New with cleansing fires, as they have done for centuries.

'Swinging the Fireballs' takes place at Stonehaven, Grampian. Flaming balls of burning rope fly round, farmers 'shoot out the Old Year' and hospitality is lavish. At Comrie, Tayside, they throw charred brands, said to contain evil spirits, into the river. At Burghead, Grampian, they 'Burn the Clavie' on Old New Year's Eve (11th January). The 'clavie' (half a tar barrel), fixed to a pole called the 'spoke', is lighted and carried round the town by the Clavie King. House doors stand open for luck. Finally, the clavie is fixed to an ancient stone altar nearby and hacked to pieces by the

King; the burned fragments are scrambled for as good luck charms. These, hung in the chimney, will keep witches and evil spirits out during the year ahead.

Similar ceremonies take place elsewhere, including Allendale (see page 97), Northumberland, and Biggar, Strathclyde.

Murdering the Old Year

The famous *Weihnachtschützen des Berchtesgadener Landes* (Berchtesgaden Christmas Shooters) is a shooting club whose members gather in long lines across the snow to fire volleys on various dates including Christmas, New Year's Eve and Epiphany. Every Christmas Eve the shooters fire at the hour of Midnight Mass, particularly at the Elevation of the Host. Since 1928 the association members have carried their banners in procession to their collegiate church; their picturesque uniform is cherished.

The public intention of the firing today is to honour Christ's birth but once the noise must have been made to waken sleeping harvest spirits and to banish from home and farm the demons of the long winter nights. Bellringing, too, had a similar purpose and was originally not celebratory but intended to have the same cheerful deterrent effect as the whip cracking, tin-can rattling and noisy music common at the New Year. Some churches ring a brief muffled peal for the Old Year; then, as the clock strikes, the bells break into their New Year peal. With bellringing, gun firing is widespread. Farmers in Angus, Scotland, gathered at the New Year to fire and in Philadelphia, Pennsylvania, on 31st December 'Murdering the Old Year' is the order of things, brought by immigrants from Germany. At midnight shooting starts and the city opens its windows for the discharge of blank cartridges.

In Europe the fun of New Year eclipses that of Christmas Day. In Amsterdam the New Year fireworks begin in mid afternoon. In Copenhagen dinner comes first, then games, fireworks and the final lighting of the tree at midnight. It is a mischief night. Bicycles are found on the roof next morning, gates on the flagpole. Moscow citizens watch spectacular fireworks behind the Spassky Tower of the Kremlin.

Presents and foods

The Romans called New Year gifts *strenae*. Tatius, king of the Sabines, was given branches from the goddess Strenia's groves and present-giving arose from this. In France New Year's Day, *le jour d'étrennes* or 'present day', is of far greater importance than Christmas. Restaurants plan luxury menus for this day with oysters, stuffed goose and *marrons glacés*. On this day stockings are filled and families visit extensively, ending with a festive evening meal with the head of the family. In Brittany the pleasant greeting of the day is: 'I wish you a good year — and Paradise at the end of your days.'

In the nineteenth century French pastrycooks in the Rue des Lombards in Paris were famous for imaginatively shaped sweet-meats sent to eager customers all over France at the New Year. Every object, from churches and playhouses to bunches of carrots, hats, boots, crowns and musical instruments, even saucepans, was attempted, all with a hollow to hold *bonbons*. These confectionery skills survive in France and Belgium today.

In Greece St Basil's influence is strong. On his day, 1st January, his cake, *Vassilopitta*, is sliced, as it has been for two thousand years. Whoever finds a coin in his or her slice will get the luck. The accompanying feast is as lavish as the family can afford; imitative magic secures a year of plenty. The table must be laden and stay so all day. In cities like Athens the cake, of milk, eggs, butter and sugar, round and marked with the date of the new year, has come from the confectioner.

In villages it is home-made, spicier and more decorative, with a coin, leaf and piece of straw inside. The leaf-finder will inherit the vineyard and the straw reveals a future farmer. The head of the household solemnly cuts the cake, the first slice for St Basil, the second for Christ, the third for the house, a slice for each family member, one for the cattle and one for the poor.

A New Year link, perhaps the last, between the Dutch settlers of Manhattan and modern American manners, just survives. Until the late nineteenth century, Dutch families of New York, following the custom of Holland, observed 'open house' on the afternoon of New Year's day, when friends and acquaintances might walk in and enjoy hospitality. Even respectable strangers passing through town might find themselves drawn through a front door and into a gathering. Sadly, modern concern for security has limited this open-handed gesture.

Balls and music

Elegant New Year balls, part of the Viennese tradition, include the *Fleckerl*, the famous but difficult left-handed waltz. But there is no excuse for ignorance; waltzing lessons are available in sev-eral languages and waltz teachers abound in Vienna.

In the Golden Hall in the Musikverein are held the Vienna Philharmonic Ball, the Flower Ball, the Confectioners', Furriers', Bakers', Doctors', Electricians' and Coffee House Owners' Balls. The *Opernball* at the Opera House is a gala occasion. At the *Jägerball* evening dress gives way to green Austrian hunting dress. Between January and March each year there are at least three

The Golden Hall of the Musikverein, Vienna, where on New Year's morning the Vienna Philharmonic Orchestra gives a Neujahrskonzert, broadcast all over the world. (Austrian National Tourist Office/ Trumler.)

hundred balls at which dancers waltz until dawn, when they drift away for soup, wine and freshly baked rolls. To begin the New Year with melody and happy memories safeguards the year to come.

On New Year's Eve, at the Hofburg Palace Imperial Ball, which recaptures the days of the Austrian Empire, a military band in the old tradition leads the dancers into the Grand Festival Hall and, as the bells of St Stephen's Cathedral ring out at midnight, toasts are drunk and the orchestra plays the 'Blue Danube' as the first waltz of the New Year.

Other countries, too, regard the New Year as dancing time. New Year balls are held in Sweden, with skating and supper parties, until 17th January, St Knut's Day, when Christmas is 'danced out'. Scots are likely to be reeling at Christmastime, when, from before Christmas into the New Year, Scottish country dancing holds the floor from Caithness to the Borders, to such tunes as 'The Duke of Perth', 'The Reel of the 51st' and 'Hamilton House'. And no consideration of balls should omit the traditional annual 'Cowboys' Ball' at Anson, Texas, an unforgettable occasion of fiddles, polkas, *schottisches* and Wild West gear, held annually since the 1880s.

Among the many concerts given in Vienna, the New Year concert by the Vienna Philharmonic Orchestra is familiar to television audiences round the world. The magnificent setting of the Golden Hall of the *Musikverein*, superbly decorated with flowers and leaves, is filled to capacity by the smartly dressed audience, who may have booked their seats up to a year in advance, so intense is the demand for places. The programme includes music of characteristic Viennese gaiety and charm. A typical programme might include music by the Strausses, father and sons, such as 'The Village Swallows', 'The Excursion Train Polka' and especially 'The Blue Danube', which typifies Vienna and traditionally welcomes the New Year. It is played everywhere; in restaurants, in hotels and on innumerable occasions of the season. Another favourite is 'The Radetzky March'.

Many of the audience will have spent the night in St Stephen's Square seeing the New Year in, while the bells of the cathedral sent out their message. By tradition stalls set up round the square to sell souvenirs offer lucky pig mascots. Also purveying luck are chimney-sweeps in working rig, who pass among the crowd offering kisses — for luck. (Black faces, like the guisers' offer powerful magic.) In the 1930s the sweeps carried squealing sucking pigs under their arms and, as they passed through the restaurants, sold bristles to diners for New Year luck.

Superstitions

'Good beginnings, good endings' and *Anfang gut, alles gut* are relevant to starting the New Year as you wish to go on. Imitative magic requires money in the pocket, a good dinner under the belt, early rising, all debts paid, a clean house with chimneys swept and nothing on loan on 1st January. People only reluctantly allowed anything to leave the house lest luck depart:

Take out, then take in, bad luck will begin;
Take in, then take out, good luck will come about,

was the correct view. This belief covered materials as mundane as potato peelings, washing water and ashes. Every visitor must

101

bring something in to preserve the family's prosperity: even a stick snatched from a handy woodpile would do. In the Ozarks people liked to open their windows for a few minutes just before midnight to let bad luck out and good luck in. Behaviour on 1st January governed the year: drunkards tried hard to keep sober. Old timers had been seen sitting in bars, watches in hand, whisky jugs before them, waiting for midnight on 1st/2nd January and release. It was wise to be busy: nothing accomplished meant a tendency to be 'idlesome' for the next twelve months. Money was slipped into the pocket of even the smallest child to ensure wealth. Bread must be newly baked for the New Year and the pantry swept clear of 'last year's crumbs'.

The doctrine of fresh starts is lively in Rome. At midnight citizens throw from their windows into the street all the old junk they can find in the house. The quantity is sufficient to make walking or car parking difficult, even dangerous. Pedestrians must keep an eye open for flying garbage but scavengers and collectors have a splendid time.

Water customs

In Greece, to ensure a 'renewal of water', all pitchers and jugs in the house on New Year's Day (St Basil's Day) must be replenished with 'new' water, freshly drawn. This 'St Basil's Water' was formerly drawn with suitable offerings to the deities of the well. Later pious references to the 'Water of Life' were another move by the church to blend pagan beliefs acceptably with Christianity.

Welsh children carrying green branches sprinkled all those they met, and on request rooms and their inmates too, to the words:

> Here we bring new water
> From the well so clear
> For to worship God with
> This happy New Year.

It was a Herefordshire custom to rush to the well at midnight to draw the first jugful of water, the 'cream of the well', considered beautifying and lucky. The maid who carried it to her mistress would be rewarded. The water was preserved as a beauty treatment and for use against witchcraft.

13
TWELFTH NIGHT AND EPIPHANY

The Three Kings

Twelfth Night, 5th January, long known for its revels (Shakespeare's play of title was written for this night), and the feast of the Epiphany, Old Christmas Day, 6th January, are the final events of Christmas, although the religious season does not end until Candlemas. The merriment and entertainments of Twelfth Night owed their character to the indulgences of *Saturnalia*. Epiphany is a more serious day dominated by the arrival in Bethlehem of the Three Kings, or Magi, bringing gifts to the infant Christ. Kaspar, king of Tarshish, brought myrrh, for mortality; Melchior, king of Numidia, gold, signifying kingship; Balthazar, king of Chaldea, frankincese, for divinity. A service is held in the Chapel Royal, St James's Palace, London, to commemorate the gifts. Offerings are made on behalf of Queen Elizabeth II. Her gift of gold is distributed to the poor; the frankincense is for church use and the myrrh goes to a hospital. Legend records that St Joseph used the gold to pay the inn's bill, burned the incense to quell the stable smells and anointed the Holy Child with myrrh against disease. Cologne

'The Three Kings and Their Presents' — 'Les Rois Mages et leur présents': marionette crib figures in the traditional tall Liège style. (Musée de la Vie Wallonne, Liège.)

'Star Singers' dressed as Magi, seen in the streets of the Old City district of Lucerne in Switzerland. (Swiss National Tourist Office/Switzerland.)

Cathedral holds the relics of the Magi in a golden shrine and, at a special Epiphany service, the *Kaiserglocke*, the Emperor's Bell, the largest in Germany, is rung.

In the home on Three Kings' Day (*Dreikönigstag*) many families add the figures of the Kings to the crib. To simulate their travels, the figures may be moved slowly inwards from the room's corners during the preceding weeks.

In many European countries, from Scandinavia to Romania, 'Star Boys' or 'Sternsingers' are to be seen in the street. Boys dressed as Magi, with gold paper crowns and carrying a lighted star lantern on a pole to commemorate the Bethlehem Star, tour the villages singing carols and collecting gifts. In the Tirol the Star Boys were encouraged to stamp on the snowy fields to benefit future crops — sure evidence of the antiquity of the custom.

There is no comparable custom in England, but Wirt Sykes, United States Consul to Wales in 1880 and a keen folklorist, found that miners visited neighbours on Christmas Eve, carrying a board stuck with lighted candles and called 'The Star'. The men knelt at every house and sang a carol to solicit a *Rhodd Nadolig* or Christmas gift.

Twelfth Night

It is regrettable that Twelfth Night, the Eve of Epiphany, has faded from celebrations. Until about 1850, particularly in England, Twelfth Night parties and, above all, dark, fruity and decorative Twelfth Night cakes almost eclipsed Christmas. Leigh Hunt wrote: 'Christmas Day is the morning of the season; New Year's Day the middle of it, or noon; Twelfth Night is the night brilliant with innumerable planets of Twelfth Cakes.'

Every baker in London rose early to dress his windows. The richest cakes rested on silver salvers. Rows of splendid confections filled shop windows: '… things animate and inanimate. Stars, castles, kings, carriages, dragons, trees, fish, palaces, cats, dogs, churches, lions, milkmaids, knights …' glittered with bright painted sugar. 'As thick as the hindwheel of a coach, and how *thick*!' said a gloating customer. The richness and splendour of the cake was an earnest of plenty in the year to come.

Outside a pastrycook's display on Twelfth Night in London, mischievous boys have played the traditional trick of pinning spectators' clothes together. This print shows the moment of enlightenment.

'Le Roi Boit' — 'The King Drinks', a Flemish Twelfth Night party.

Naughty boys loitering by bakers' shops took advantage of an absorbed audience to play traditional tricks; spectators' clothes were quietly pinned together, coat tails to skirt, or coat tails to window frame. Until the customers moved nothing happened; then eight or ten people might find themselves struggling, hooked together, while boys and bystanders shrieked with delight.

At Twelfth Night parties a Bean King was chosen by the finding in a slice of cake of a dried bean, and a Queen by the finding of a pea. It was a cheerful moment, echoed in a pleasant phrase for good luck used in France: *Il a trouvé la fève au gâteau*. The elections derived from the Saturnalian choice of *Rex Convivii* by lot. The two presided over the evening's amusements. In France, Germany and Austria the election is still ceremonious. Toasts are incessant. Cries of *Le roi boit* ('The king drinks') ring out. Formerly the Bean King had the privilege of paying for all refreshments. The elections were universal: in the thirteenth century even the monastery of Mont St Michel in Normandy had its Bean King.

Oxen had their own cake in farming districts. A special cake with a hole in it was baked and hung on the horns of the best ox with the words:

Fill your cups, my merry men all
For here's the best ox in the stall
O, he is the best ox, of that there's no mistake
So let us crown him with the Twelfth Cake!

The ox was encouraged to toss the cake for luck.

At Twelfth Night parties 'characters' determined partners. Printed sets of slips sold by stationers bore such names as Boarding House Lady or Mrs Squinge, Monsieur François Parley-Vous or Patrick O'Tater. Hostesses counted their invited female guests and numbered and folded slips to match. Ladies' characters were sent round in a reticule, men's in a hat, and guests arranged themselves for a jolly evening in pairs as fate had decreed.

Although the hilarity of Twelfth Night has faded, one echo remains in the ceremony of the Baddeley Cake at Drury Lane Theatre, London, on 6th January, performed each year before the company, made up and in costume, playing in the theatre at the time. Robert Baddeley (1732-94), a stage-struck pastrycook, persuaded David Garrick to let him act. Unhappily, while dressing for *School for Scandal* in 1794, Baddeley died, leaving money to provide a cake, 'along with sundry bowls of Punch to be provided by a grateful manager'. *My Fair Lady* holds the record of having cut five Baddeley cakes. Many famous actors have taken part,

The cast of 'Miss Saigon' cut the Baddeley Cake at the Theatre Royal, Drury Lane, London, in 1992. (Theatre Royal, Drury Lane.)

including Garrick, Kean, Siddons, Kemble and Irving. In 1992 the 187th cake of the series was cut by the company of *Miss Saigon*. Baddeley's choice of 6th January for his ceremony clearly links it with the Twelfth Cake custom which he must have known so well in his profession as a baker.

Blessing the Waters

In Greece and every country of the Eastern Church a special service of Blessing the Waters takes place in the Octave of Epiphany, the eight-day period beginning on 6th January. Sometimes the sea is blessed, or a river, lake or stream. The bishop often throws a cross into the water, using a ribbon to draw it out, and sprinkles those present with the flying drops of water.

At Tarpon Springs, Florida, among sponge fishers of Greek descent it is 'Greek Cross Day', when a colourful procession passes through decorated streets from the church to Spring Bayou. A gold cross is tossed into the sea by the archbishop; some thirty young divers plunge in to retrieve it and to receive a blessing.

Until the Blessing of the Waters lays them safely away, the *Kallikantzaroi* demons are the terror of the Greek peasant during the Twelve Days. Half animal and half human, black and hairy with huge heads, monkeys' arms, long fingernails, beasts' feet and bloodied tongues, the *Kallikantzaroi* are a terrifying sight. During the day they hide, to emerge at night to attack the house, leaving the inhabitants half dead with fright. Only at dawn do they depart for home. A precautionary cross on the house door on Christmas Eve, incense, the crackling Yule log and a pacifier of pork bones and sausages in the chimney are the few countermeasures a family can employ.

The principal activity of *Kallikantzaroi* is said to be felling the tree which supports the earth. At the very moment when they have nearly succeeded Christ is born, the tree grows whole again and the *Kallikantzaroi*, in a final fury, emerge determined to enter the house down the chimney. The blazing Yule log keeps them out.

Lights, fires and precautions

In Austria in the Salzkammergut the *Glöcklerlauf* (Bellringers' Procession) takes place on Epiphany Eve, 5th January, again intended to keep Alpine demons away. Large flat bells are slung on leather straps round the *Glöcklers'* shoulders and hips and attached to sticks they carry. Their tall fantastic wooden head-dresses (*Glöcklerkappen*), up to 10 feet (3 metres) long and 6 feet (1.8 metres) high and weighing up to 33 pounds (15 kg), are an unforgettable sight, covered with decorated opaque paper and lighted from within to give a stained-glass effect. To keep the huge

Decorations on a Glöckler's great head-dress (Glöcklerkappen) at Ebensee am Traunsee, Austria, include the edelweiss, gentian and other Alpine flowers. Lights shine through it to give a stained-glass effect. At the Glöckler's side hangs a great bell, which gives the procession its name of 'Bellringers'. (Ebensee am Traunsee Tourismusverband/Karl Weigl.)

Light and noise marked Holly Night at Brough, Cumbria. On Twelfth Night the townspeople carried a burning holly tree round the town with a band, torches, rockets and much cheering. The fragments were thrown to the crowd for luck and carried off to the inns.

head-dresses in place requires practice and skill. Few, if any, traditional costumes are more beautiful than the *Glöcklers'*, typified by those to be seen in the village of Ebensee am Traunsee, which are decorated with local flowers such as the edelweiss and gentian and local scenes such as the watermill.

Christmas is a season of lights and fire and this is never more apparent than in the little town of Pottenstein on the river Püttlach in Franconia, southern Germany. The town celebrates *Dreikönigstag*, Three Kings' Day, or Epiphany, with a great torchlight procession and festival of lights. The steep surrounding cliffs and hills with the dominating tenth-century castle, fine timbered houses and the nearby Teufelshöhle (or Devil's Cave) are bathed in flickering light from hundreds of bonfires and thousands of torches, which gather brilliance from the surrounding snow. It is a sea of light impressive enough to drive away any lurking demon.

On the Eve of Epiphany the *Perchtenlauf* or *Berchtenlauf* makes its way through the Alpine villages. *Perchten* are double-edged demons, half inimical, half beneficial if encouraged to dance on the fields. They can be good or evil, ugly or beautiful in appearance. Often there are as many as two or three hundred persons in the run, all masked, with cowbells and sticks, shouting and running to knock on doors to drive away spirits. In Salzburg they are called *Schnabel Perchten* ('Beaked *Perchten*') and wear old clothes and huge cloth beaks. They carry brooms for sweeping, scissors to cut open the slovenly and let the dirt in (or perhaps out) and crates for the transport of the incorrigible. Ugly *Perchten* are dressed in skins and horned masks but the beautiful are noted for the tranquillity and serenity of their expressions.

Until the nineteenth century young people in the apple-growing regions of Normandy marched round the orchards on Epiphany with blazing torches, intent on disposing by magic of moles, caterpillars and possibly less tangible enemies also. Younger children assisted by lighting hay wisps.

Bavarian farms may still be protected with a chalk inscription on the door lintel showing the Three Kings' initials and the year: '19 K + M + B 92'. Once the priest blessed the chalk before the task began. In clean country air the marks often last for the full year.

In Bohemia, too, three crosses were made on every door in the

Pottenstein, Franconia, holds its Lichterfest ('Festival of Lights') on Three Kings' Day, 6th January, each year. There is a torchlight procession and cliffs and surrounding hills are ablaze with light. (Städisches Verkehrsbüro, Pottenstein.)

On the Eve of Epiphany Perchten move through Austrian villages; these are at Imst in the Tirol. They can be good or evil; Schönperchten, like these, are benign and famous for their serenity of expression. (Austrian National Tourist Office/Hubmann.)

house, inside and out, barn, stable, cowshed, dog kennel and hen coop. No witch might pass through. Bonfires roared reassuringly skywards and besom brooms of twigs were thrown high to represent the destruction and scattering of witches. Anyone foolish enough to point at a flying broom would find his fingers burned.

It was another *Rauchnacht* in southern Germany and Austria, where on Epiphany Eve the thoughtful family sat round to snuff up the fumes from a dish of burning frankincense to keep diseases away from the year. Everyone was purified by the sacred smoke from the censer while the peasant's wife sprinkled every room, person and animal, with holy water.

Farewell to Christmas

Christmas is nearly over in the worldly sense although, ecclesiastically, it lasts until Candlemas. On Saint Distaff's Day, 7th January, the women returned to spinning after the holiday. It was a light-hearted return to reality; the men tried to burn the girls' flax and the girls drenched the men with buckets of water:

> Bring in pails of water then,
> Let the maids bewash the men,

The traditional ceremony of Blessing the Plough on Plough Sunday at Chichester Cathedral, West Sussex. (R. D. Barrett-Lennard.)

> Give Saint Distaff all the right,
> Then bid Christmas sport *Goodnight*!

sang Robert Herrick.

Then it was the turn of the men. On Plough Monday, the first Monday after Twelfth Day, blowing cowhorns and wearing beribboned mumming costumes, the ploughmen, 'plough Jacks' or 'Plough Stots', went out, dragging a plough with them. In the play at Revesby, Lincolnshire, characters included the Fool's Sons, Pickle Herring, Blue Breeches, Pepper Breeches and Ginger Breeches. They locked swords round the Fool's (their father's) neck, then with a clatter sprang aside. The Fool lay dead.

> Good people all, you see what we have done.
> We have cut down our father like the evening sun,
> He lies here in all his purple gore
> And we are afraid he will never dance more.

But at the stamp of a foot the Fool jumps up restored. Until the Reformation money collected during this frolic paid to keep the 'plough light' burning in the village church.

Calvados, Normandy, too, had its final ceremonies directed towards the famous apple orchards. On Twelfth Day peasants jumped through the cleansing smoke of bonfires shouting their farewell to Christmas and the Three Kings.

The Plough Monday procession.

Further Reading

Alford, Violet. *The Hobby Horse and Other Animal Masks.* Merlin, 1978.

Auld, William Muir. *Christmas.* Macmillan, 1931.

Barnett, J. H. *The American Christmas.* Macmillan, 1954.

Dawson, W. F. *Christmas, Its Origins and Associations.* Elliot Stock, 1902.

Ettlinger, L. D., and Holloway, R. G. *Compliments of the Season.* Penguin, 1947.

Hadfield, Miles and John. *The Twelve Days of Christmas.* Cassell, 1961.

Hole, C. *Christmas and Its Customs.* Bell, 1953.

James, E. *Seasonal Feasts and Festivals.* Thames & Hudson, 1961.

Miles, Clement A. *Christmas in Ritual and Tradition.* T. Fisher Unwin, 1912.

The Oxford Book of Carols, Oxford University Press, 1983.

Sanson, William. *Christmas.* Weidenfeld & Nicholson, 1968.

Shauffler, Robert Haven. *Christmas.* Dodd Mead, 1930.

Wenecke, Herbert H. *Christmas Customs around the World.* Bailey, 1974.

Whistler, Lawrence. *The English Festivals.* 1947.

Folklore (formerly *Folk-lore*, formerly *Folk-lore Journal*).
Journal of American Folklore.
Notes and Queries.

INDEX

Place-names appear under countries and in some cases individually also.
Page numbers in italics refer to illustrations.